THE LIGHT OF THE SPIRIT

An Introductory Guide

Mary Bassano

SAMUEL WEISER, INC.

York Beach, Maine

First published in 1996 by
Samuel Weiser, Inc.
Box 612
York Beach, ME 03910-0612

Library of Congress Cataloging-in-Publication Data

Bassano, Mary
    The light of the spirit: an introductory guide / Mary Bassano.
        p.   cm.
    Includes bibliographical references.
    (alk. paper)
        1. Light—Religious aspects.   2. Light—Psychological aspects.
3. spiritual life.   I. Title.
BL265.L5B67   1996
291.2'12—dc20   96-13474
                                                                     CIP

ISBN 0-87728-871-2
CCP

Typeset in Benguiat

Cover art is "Wolkentor," Copyright © 1996 Klaus Holitzka. Walter Holl Agency, Germany.

Printed in the United States of America

02   01   00   99   98   97   96
10   9   8   7   6   5   4   3   2   1

The paper used in this publication meets the minimum requirements of the American National Standard for Permanence of Paper of Printed Library Materials Z39.48-1984.

Contents

FOREWORD

Mary Bassano is one of those people who glow. Her smile lights up the faces around her. You feel the warmth, just being in the same room. When I first met Mary, my mother had just moved to a new apartment and I was being introduced to a new friend. I knew immediately that this would be a person with whom Mama could share her thoughts and feelings—especially her love of music and art. They didn't always agree, but the love and light kept them good friends until Mother's death. Mary shares her light with many others and people who know her know that this inner light sustains and strengthens her daily activities, her writing, and her teaching. I am really grateful that Mama shared Mary with me.

—Virginia Dory

Acknowledgments

I wish to express deep appreciation to everyone who has helped me while I was writing this book. My thanks to Holly Morgan, who first encouraged and inspired me; to Dr. Wang Pachow, a Buddhist and Professor of Religion, for his contributions to the information on light of Buddhism; to Rabbi Lipsker for his contribution to the material regarding the light of Judaism; to Sheila Spafford for her help with the manuscript; and to Susan Kreider for her additional work, and for information regarding the Baha'i faith.

I send joy and gratitude to those friends who have given me love, help, and inspiration.

I behold you all in the Light!

Introduction

We may ask ourselves, "What is the true meaning of Light? What is it?" Light is, indeed, a mysterious, illusive "thing"—an interesting phenomenon. It is a gift. It is an intangible energy, yet one that opens the way, not only to "see," but to experience truth, wisdom, and knowledge.

Down through the ages philosophers and scientists have perceived light to be many things, both spiritual and material, and have searched for its source from the sun, moon, stars, and God. Today we also realize that there is a spiritual energy within physical electrical vibrations. However, "the sighted eye requires more than the input of natural light; it also requires Empedocles' (the Greek philosopher's) inner, ocular light of intelligence; if we neglect the animating light of coherent intelligence that illumines and flows through all our senses, then the glory of the world stands mute before our inquiring spirit."[1]

There are many words that describe light because it is operative on so many diverse levels—photons, laser beams, rainbows, the light of the sun, the invisible vibration of light waves moving throughout the omniverse. Is it not fascinating

---

[1] Arthur Zajonc, *Catching the Light* (New York: Bantam, 1993), p. 205.

to observe the light of a star which may continue to travel toward us long after the star has disintegrated? Then there is the aura, the light that reflects from humans, animals, and all forms of nature. The more we look, the deeper our awareness and respect for the great Divine Power behind all the activities and energies in our universe.

Do we recognize ourselves as Beings of Light? Do we SEE the Light of God? Our eyes reflect the soul. As we learn to look deeply into our eyes, we begin to see and experience something beyond the physical.

Do you feel you are a contributor to the healing process of our Planet Earth? This planet is your home, whether you leave it tomorrow or not. Even if you have come from another world, this is your home *now*, and you are responsible for bringing it into the light. As we were told, "Ye are the light of the world."[2]

Let us begin to explore all the avenues of light—physical, electrical, animal, human, angelic, the light of the subtle body, the light of pure Spirit. We will work with many dimensions brought to our attention by scientists, philosophers, photographers, masters, and work with our own discoveries. We will delve deeply into this intricate subject of LIGHT; investigate its many facets, and learn how we can become ONE with it. With its strength and spirituality we can become receptive

---

[2] Holy Bible, The King James Version (Oxford Co New York: Oxford University Press), Matthew 5:14.

to its power to develop our minds, our inner seeing, and can recognize its wondertul healing properties on both physical and mental levels.

Hopefully this book will open new doors for understanding the significance and need for light in our lives.

CHAPTER 1

LIGHT ANSWERS

Many questions have been asked about light. The easiest way to begin our exploration is to ask some basic questions. These questions come from a store of questions I have answered over the years when I have been teaching classes.

One question I have heard is how to reconcile the difference between the physics of light and the perception of light as a spiritual phenomenon. We are told that light came forth to create the Universe. Within this great light are innumerable variations of vibrational energies which emanate from the One Source. Even though there are differences in the application, appearance, and vibrations (as in humans), nevertheless the universal assumption is that there is but *one* light.

From a scientific viewpoint, Benjamin Franklin's discovery of electricity, those unexpected

vibrational energies, were actually made known to
him through his experimentation with the kite. He
quickly made use of this "finding," and from his discovery of what was already there, the field of elec-
tronics grew rapidly (and is still expanding) in
countless ways. Our *perception* of spiritual light
may appear to be in opposition to, or different
from, the light coming from an electric bulb, but in
essence, it is all coming from the same source.

In order to reconcile the differences between
physical and spiritual light, we must accept the fact
that so-called differences are a result of how we
use the energy. True, we gain light from the physical body we call the sun, but it, too, as the Earth,
was first created by some universal "force" which
we call the Divine Light, thus making spiritual energy the basis and reality of all physical forms and
bodies.

Reconciliation is actually the understanding of
the multiple aspects of the One, just as a magnetic
pole varies from negative to positive but is nevertheless *one* substance.

I have been queried as to why darkness is associated with evil, and light with good. Darkness is
often incorrectly associated with evil as it prevents
one from seeing; fear develops due to the un-
known, and fear is the basis of all negativity. There
is another side to darkness, however. Please refer
to chapter 4, "Darkness and Light."

Light is related to good for when earthly situations are exposed to the light, they are then "seen"
with clarity; darkness evaporates and light brings an
upliftment in the consciousness. Since light is of

God, it can point the way to good. Please refer to chapter 2, "What is Light?" With people who have a high consciousness, this light appears as a halo around them.

Everyone has a light within. It will radiate forth and surround the body only when we are functioning on a high spiritual level. The consciousness-state is the switch which turns on that inner light so it shines outwardly to the degree of our spiritual awareness. Each one of us has such a light; as we radiate forth our love, compassion, and truth, so do we light all around us.

Many people wonder where or what the true origin of light is, and how it affects us. Light comes from the one source of all—the Omniversal Power, Strength, and Love. We may assume that our light originates from the sun, which it does, but the sun, itself, was first created from that great, original Cause. Light affects us in many diverse ways, depending on our needs, our willingness to "receive," and our level of consciousness. Please refer to chapter 6, "How Do We Use Light Energies?"

Light can also produce different colors when it penetrates a prism and breaks up the various rays, thus resulting in the differences in colors. *Webster's 9th Collegiate Dictionary* says that color is a property of reflection. It is a phenomenon of light or visual perception that enables one to differentiate otherwise identical objects. For example, when light emits a radiance through raindrops, we perceive a rainbow—a reflection of light producing different colors. Light filtering into a glass of water also produces colors. The amount of brilliance of

light going through any of these receptors deter-
mines the value, hue and intensity of colors.

The growth of the retina of the eyes is responsible for the receptivity of not only the seven spectrum colors, but also their blends, tints, and hues.
Eons ago, human beings could distinguish only two
or three colors, but as the human body evolved,
the retina became cognizant of more and more colors within all of nature. As our "seeing" continues
to develop, we will become aware of ever more brilliant colors, not merely on the physical plane, but
also on the more subtle planes as well.

We are most certainly in need of light; indeed,
we might even call light the "breath of life." Light is
the one nutrient without which we could no longer
exist. It enables us to see, not only on the physical
level, but to *see*, i.e., to learn and acknowledge the
great mysteries of Wisdom and Truth. It points the
way.

There are ways in which we react to light. Light,
as with many things of the spirit, vibrates on such a
high level that it is too powerful for some people to
endure. There are those who cannot handle extreme
sunlight on a physical level; others fear *pure* light as
it reveals the dark areas of their lives. Many prefer
darkness, as it is a "hiding place." To truly receive
light is being willing to open oneself to find TRUTH.

On a physical level, if not careful, we can be
blinded by the bright glare from the sun. Likewise,
on a spiritual level, we can be overcome by the illumination of a great Master. However, as we grow
and prepare ourselves, our reaction and receptivity
to light in every way will become more positive, and

we will develop understanding as to our acceptance of it.

There are various meanings of light for those who are blind. As one such person related (although not blind from birth)—she perceives light as a heavy, thick fog. Sometimes everything will be completely black, then all seems white, somewhat like "snow blindness." In a room where there is no window, she may suddenly see a blob of light similar to a window, and in another room, cartons appear to be piled all over. She may "see" articles on a table at one moment, and in the next, they are gone. The eyes may act as a camera, taking pictures which may then be recorded. However, if anything is "seen," it is an aberration. These experiences would, of course, vary depending on the degree of blindness. Many blind people have developed such sensitivities that the *presence* of light may be felt even when not seen.

The third eye is the frontal center situated behind the brow and between the two physical eyes. It is called our center of higher vision. When light gets to the third eye, awareness is raised from the psychic to the spiritual level. Light may enter the third eye only when we recognize the third eye's importance—that it is the seat of intuition and insight. When we *know* that this deep, intuitive Self (God) is available if we would open ourselves to it in faith and trust, then the light enters and opens the path for us. It is as if we were previously living in a room with locked doors, observing life on quite a limited level. Then, as we realize we can unlock these doors and step out into the fullness of light, we suddenly acknowledge the vastness and awakening possibilities and we allow our spiritual receptors to come forth. Please refer to chapter 13, "Seeing Through the Windows of the Soul." This is analogous to working on the psychic or lower astral plane where there are limitations to our seeing and experiencing; we are closeted in "one room" where we may be vulnerable to possible negative influences. If we become cognizant of higher levels of consciousness and put forth a desire to rise above the lower astral plane, then the door will unlock of itself, and we will be shown the majesty and divine splendor of the higher and more pure spiritual plane. Our awareness will become receptive to the guidance of the Masters and our "seeing" will be greatly enhanced. We know we can trust that quiet Inner Voice and we move forward in peace and trust.

CHAPTER 2

WHAT IS LIGHT?

Light is Life. It is Spirit. We all have the potential to use the light within, if we would but allow ourselves to see. "The only thing that prevents it is your unwillingness to drop what you have come to believe is a state or condition. Drop the veil and behold, there is the light."[1]

Light is a "many splendoured thing." "Perhaps light is a singing flame, a delicate vibration of the luminiferous ether."[2]

Luminescence is in everything, for it represents light itself. As we develop our inner seeing, we may often observe this light radiation, which projects forth from all forms of wildlife, as well as

---

[1] Baird Spalding, *Life and Teachings of the Masters of the Far East,* Vol. IV (Marina del Rey, CA: DeVorss, 1924), p. 159.
[2] Arthur Zajonc, *Catching the Light* (New York: Bantam, 1993), p. 105.

from humans, depending on the human levels of consciousness and growth. As James Redfield explains in his book, *The Celestine Prophecy,* we can develop our "seeing" of this powerful glowing by first observing the energy and beauty—the God life—in trees, flowers, in all of nature and in mankind.

This illumination in our world proves the Oneness of everything in our universe. According to quantum physics, the light of the most minute atom connects with the light of the farthest star in the most distant galaxy.

Light by and of itself is invisible. We cannot "see" light unless it has an object (such as the retina) on which to shine. Is this not similar to the theory of a tree falling in the forest when there is no one to hear, and thus, makes no sound? Light is life itself. We would have no life without this great spiritual energy. As Goethe said, *"You* would not exist if the light did not see *you!"*[3]

We cannot, at this point in our development, endure the full glow of light; we cannot comprehend it, nor can our bodies withstand the extremely high vibrations. However, as we continue on the upward path, we will develop our spiritual sensitivity and gradually be able to absorb more and more of this eternal, divine vibratory energy.

No matter how brilliant the day, if we lack that formative, artistic power of imagination, we become blind, both figuratively

---

[3] Arthur Zajonc, *Catching the Light,* p. 340.

and literally. We need the light within as well as daylight for vision.[4]

We have within us a natural divine guidance that will direct us where, when, and how we should proceed. We do not need to ask for light to lead us; just give thanks, for it is already there! It is as natural for *us* to realize its presence as it is for animals and birds who have an innate instinct for this inner guidance. "If we pray to God 'out there' for light and guidance, our prayer may actually block out the flow of light and guidance from within."[5] We need to listen and receive. Light is always with us. "Be still, and know that I am God" (Psalms 46:10).

It is necessary to become quiet to tune in to this light which is a true reality within, before attempting the next step on the path. Feel the effusion of light, *allow* it to pour forth, and you will begin to see the way. If you do not sense the radiation, ask yourself in all honesty, "What blocks am I putting up that hinders this flow of light?" You must learn to let go of the pressure of making decisions, for example. Just let go, be still, and you will find the answer within you, as it is always there. Knowledge is within. We need only to awaken, see it, and be willing to accept it.

What is divine guidance but the flow of light that emanates through you as you release the barriers and give it freedom to flow The light is here,

---

[4] *Catching the Light*, p. 12.
[5] Eric Butterworth, *In the Flow of Life* (Castro Valley, CA: Unity Books, 1982), p. 40.

now and always. Do you not feel it, see it, and know it is here? Do you have expectations for the truth of the insights you receive? *Expect,* do not doubt. Feel that guidance that is yours to receive. Lift up your consciousness and see the light at the end of the tunnel.

Light is a multi-dimensional spiritual/physical energy creating waves that brought our universe into manifestation. It has created, and is continually creating, all forms of life. We continue to evolve because of the great power flow of our sun. This light from the sun is life itself, giving not only physical vitality, but mental and spiritual strength, and a sense of joy. We are not always aware of this direction of energy, but the more cognizant of it we become, the more use we will have of this great power.

> Light enters the eyes not only to serve vision, but to go directly to the body's biological clock within the hypothalamus—the hypothalamus acts as a puppet master who, quietly and out of sight, controls most of the functions that keep the body in balance.[6]

Light is not something that we can pick up in our hands and hold, yet it is everywhere. Without it, we could see nothing. We are living and moving in it constantly. The sun may go down and the darkness

---

[6] Jacob Liberman, *Light: Medicine of the Future* (Santa Fe: Bear & Co., 1991), p. 35

arrive, but the energy is still there. As we turn on the electric switch to bring light into a darkened room, so can we transmute the inner darkness in our lives into light. This light is the threshold of all things enabling sight, expansion of knowledge, strength, courage, and wisdom. We are able to turn on the electricity in our houses, and we can also "turn on the switch" of our inner self to bring forth that great divine understanding.

Light is a force; Light is God; and God is Light. This vibrant energy not only surrounds us, it is within us, and we are in it. Light emanates from us in limitless ways, but only as our thoughts direct these vibrations can light be effective. The source is God, or pure light and love. This intangible energy in our lives is the true reality of our being. As our consciousness becomes more and more enlightened, then we grow in our awareness and receptivity to the light.

We know that our bodies, both physical and subtle, radiate light. Jacob Liberman talks about this light body when he discusses how our pineal gland works. "The ability of the pineal to determine whether it is light or dark outside . . . thus tells the body when to work and when to rest, (and) allows our biological rhythms to occur smoothly. We truly are light bodies."[7] This divine light of which he speaks truly brings us wisdom and truth, and leads us to our freedom of spirit.

The great illumined Masters knew the value and power of this wonderful light energy. They could

[7] Jacob Liberman, *Light: Medicine of the Future*, p. 32.

heal and protect with it; they could open doors to
spiritual planes of life, showing us that the veil can
be torn aside if we let loose our barriers.

Let's look again at this inner light that
emanates from us. It is referred to as the aura. We
all have an aura. Its brightness relates to the degree
of our spirituality. We shine forth light and truth as
we grow within. The greater our awakening, the
greater the illumination radiating from us. This effusion of light is not readily recognized by the average person. Those who do see the aura usually
have clairvoyant abilities. It can be helpful to a
healer, for instance, to be able to see the aura and
to comprehend its significance. The various colors
of the aura, and their intensities in the auric field
can indicate imbalances that can aid in diagnosing
mental and physical conditions.

This etheric energy is also called the Pranic
Light which represents the true light of spiritual
illumination—the highest vibration. It is far and
beyond the psychic realm, above the lower astral
plane, and is "seen" only through the single or
third eye. This pranic energy may often be
termed "pranayama," pranic waves in which there
are waves of light similar to the seven spectrum
colors.

Light is now being recognized as one of the
greatest energies in the prevention and healing of
dis-ease. We are truly spiritual beings with this
Divine Light energy within. It is important to understand that we may become healing helpers to one
another and to our entire planet. We know that "sci-
ence has long recognized light's importance to

plants and animals; its human application is recent—in addition to treating cancer and body-clock disturbances, light is being enlisted to fight emotional disorders. Growing evidence suggests that seasonal variations in light levels can have a profound impact on mental health."[8]

"Light is a symbol of intelligence. We cannot affirm too often, 'I am intelligence; I am the light of my world,' "[9] Yes, light is wisdom, intelligence, truth and power. It is an energy for healing and protection.

Manifestations of genius and creativity are all expressions of the light that is within, radiating outward. This light is also recognized in the seemingly unnoticed acts of daily living. The light may come forth with a simple gesture, an act of kindness, a word of faith and love. According to our life's actions and attitudes, so does our light shine. Without the pouring forth of Divine Light, there would be no planet Earth, no universe and no you and me. "And God said, 'Let there be Light' and there was Light" (Genesis 1:3). This was the creative vibration that brought life in all its myriad forms into manifestation. It continues to stay with us as a nourishing energy.

If we center ourselves in a bubble of pure light, releasing all tensions and fears, then we become receptive to that which we wish to create. Words and ideas will pour into us as we patiently wait. Too

---

[8] Stephen Rae, "Bright Light, Big Therapy," in *Modern Maturity*, February-March, 1994, p. 84.
[9] *Metaphysical Bible Dictionary* (Unity), p. 403.

often we are in a hurry, or allow ourselves to be stressed, and block the way for inspiration and creativity to come forth.

Talents often lie hidden within us; sometimes we fear to face them. Often low self-esteem and a lack of confidence are uppermost in our minds, and we are unable or unwilling to accept all the abilities and resources with which we are endowed. Surrounding ourselves in the light enables us to think. Action and creativity follows thought. Light is the initial creative power and so it continues to be. It opens our eyes to imaging, and imagination creates. Our dreams and imaginings come from the light.

Light is a protective shield if we truly understand this concept. Down through the ages we have been taught about God's presence, which is constantly with us and *is* our source of protection. We must have faith in this great spiritual essence, so that we may *feel* and accept this protective energy. Visualizing this light around us creates an unfoldment of spiritual consciousness, and "seeing" the light on the path ahead of us gives further comfort, guidance and a feeling of safety. Whenever we have fears of any kind, we must release them all to this great light of spirituality. No matter where we may be in our lives, this light will always be there. All we need to do is to open our minds and hearts, and receive!

Let's examine some of the physical and mental aspects of light. Light is, according to *Funk & Wagnall's Standard College Dictionary*, the form of radiant energy that stimulates the organs of sight, having for normal human vision, wave length rangaing from about 3900 to 7700 angstroms and travelaing at a speed of about 186,300 miles per secaond—it is also mental or spiritual understanding or insight; enlightenment—as well as being the state of being unhidden and observable; to "come to light." And although it may not be externally visible, it is the spiritual or "inner" light, and its velocity is instant presence.

We should express gratitude and give praise to the sun which, although radiating physical energy to lighten our path, is also emitting spiritual rays, since the sun is truly a living, spiritual entity, as is our planet Earth. In early Egyptian days, sunlight was presumed to have emanated from the Sun God, Ra. We should acknowledge the value of our sun in our lives, as it gives us essential energies. For instance, we energize our food and water through the application of light, as light itself is a necessary nutrient. However, merely being out in the light *ourselves* can nourish and energize us.

Another source of light comes from electrical units. According to *Webster's New World Dictionary*, electricity is a "property of certain fundamental paraticles of all matter, as electrons (negative charges) and protons (positive charges)." Yes, electricity is matter which is a part of universal substance. Electricity was not invented by Ben Franklin, it was "discovered." Since this light source has always been present since the days of creation, we now know that light is ever here, but we must make the effort to tap into it, to find it, to recognize its posiative value. Since this discovery and consequent inventions, we, to a degree, control "material light." Can we, as well, learn to control and use the inner light of wisdom, love, and knowledge?

As we begin to understand the correlation of this so-called physical light with vibrational energies of universal matter, do we not see that all matter is truly of spiritual substance, and that spiritual energies impregnate matter? ALL IS ONE, and everything manifests according to its individual nature and purpose.

We react to physical light in our surroundings, and so do plants, animals, and most life forms. "There is some speculation that certain migrating birds may also respond to this quality of light."[10] Birds, however, do not emit light, nor do leafy plants, although it has been said that with clairvoyant vision some people have seen light emitting from *all* forms of nature. It has also been reported that certain kinds of fish send forth a so-called luminescence, or living light. Have you heard that due to the ability of fireflies to shine forth light, lanterns containing these fireflies have been made?

There are so many great and interesting manifestations of light, and one of the greatest surprises that came from exploring light was the development of photography—the idea that light could be used to reproduce an image on a photographic plate and, depending on a projection of light, the images could change! As a local photographer, Virginia Dory, explained, the real purpose of pho-

---

[10] *Academic American Encyclopedia* (Danbury, CT: Grolier Electronic Publisher, 1995).

tography is to "tell a story." The photographer needs to find the story in the subject, and use the tools of artistic composition to focus upon it. The special tool of the photographer is the light—natural or artificial—used to elaborate and focus upon the story. As the picture is developed, the meaning of the story is brought forth. External and physically manipulated light can produce wonders if applied intelligently and with a meaningful goal. This is also true of our application of spiritual light. So, another use of light is to tell the story!

CHAPTER 3

LIGHT LEADS US TO TRUTH AND FREEDOM

How do we free ourselves from the material and physical boundaries that we place around us? We do it by filling our Beings with true Light—the Light that will point the way—the Light of the Divine Spirit within ourselves. Once we have realized that this power of wisdom and energy is part of our own being, then we can begin to follow the path that leads to freedom. If we want to heal the dis-ease or blocks we have created, we must recognize the light as a medicinal energy which, when applied properly, can smooth out imbalances and bring harmony to the soul.

How do we do this? First, by recognizing its power and then by learning how to use it. We are our own "Lamp-Lighters." The light is always there; it lights up the whole body; every atom and cell is filled with it.

One of the most important ways to become fully aware of this great power within us is by turning within during meditation; to SEE this light with the inner eye; to FEEL it flowing through our entire being, and to BREATHE it into our very soul. To do this, we must first LET GO of our little selves and let the inner Self—the God within—lead the way. We must quiet the ego and surrender to Divine Spirit by completely releasing worry, fear, and any of the many negatives that we have allowed to surround us.

Now, as we "let go," visualize a little light switch behind the heart. Reach in mentally, and turn it on one degree. As you do so, you will feel and visualize the light flowing through you, bringing life and healing to your body. Then, reach back again and turn the light up once more. Now you will feel it even more strongly. It will give you a sense of "aliveness." You will start to "open up" and become aware of your spiritual teachers and guides, who are now able to reach you, as you have opened the door. Now, for a third and last time, turn the light up once again. At this point, you will become aware of *only* the light; all else has dropped away and you know you are now One with God, the Light. You are whole and free at this moment. As you gradually come back down to your present level of living, you sense a difference. The light is still with you, and you can now face challenges with a new and greater sense of the power of light. Regardless of the duties of the day, this light will remain with you. When problems confront you, remember your experience in the light and know that this light can be yours always as you *choose* to receive it. As you continue to allow this flow of light to be one with you, you will feel a release from any bondage, regardless of outer circumstances, and you recognize the truth of this Oneness. A burden has rolled off your shoulders, and you are free!

Since you and the Creator are One, you now have control over outer influences that have, in the past, kept you from attaining your goals, from reaching out into your own creativity. You now know the full meaning of Jesus' words, "Ye shall know the Truth and the Truth shall set you free" (John 8:32). Now that we know that God resides within us, we can let go of fears, hate and worries to realize that the greatest power in the Universe is a part of our own Self!

As we continue with the knowledge of light being our creative power, let us realize that the greatest help we can give ourselves and others is to first find this light and then acknowledge its constructive guidance. We need to be aware, first, of this guiding light and then aid others in finding it. Think of the symbology of the flashlight. You may flash the light on a path for someone, but it will only be as *you* see the light on *your* path. Then it is up to the other person to find his or her own "flashlight." There is only one light, but each one manifests or accepts it according to the present level of growth and awareness.

As we beam rays of this holy light on negatives, fears, and on things of the past that may have *seemed* to destroy us, these situations will be transformed into positives, and we will begin to perceive in a completely different light. We may not forget experiences of the past, but we can and must learn to observe them from a more spiritual level of awareness. Then the ties that bind us are gone.

Another part of the process of being transmuted by the light is to know that if you truly recognize yourself as a Light Being, then you will have no need to pronounce judgment on anyone, but will merely behold others in a circle of light. You will feel better for letting go of any wish to criticize or hold contempt for another human being. People who are doing horrendous things live in darkness; and are without an awareness of the Great Spirit of Light within them. We can show compassion, rather than hate and anger, and surround others with the healing light. Sharing our energy from this positive point of view will help the planet.

As we experience the light within, we will realize that it's important to radiate this light to other humans, and to the planet, and to the Universe, too. How wonderful it is to feel the connection—the Oneness—with all humanity, with space, with nature. It's wonderful to be free enough to feel this and not allow ourselves to become enveloped by any negative vibrations.

"Perfect Love (Light) casteth out fear" (1 John 4:18). When we truly accept this, we then experience wonderful feelings of release and lightness of body and mind. Freedom is a joyous thing—to be really free of society's demands; to be free from the effects of criticism and hurts; to be free of all the guilts and traumas of this material world. This is a gigantic step upward in our spiritual evolvement. As the light points the way to our acceptance of Divine Order and Divine Justice, we can then let go of fear—fear being the basis of all negativity.

In trying to establish yourself as a free spirit, relax and try to see and feel the Universal Light of God around you and within you. Allow it to become a part of you. When we allow the light to shine forth, the path of Truth opens before us and the Truth then prepares the road to freedom. Without this awareness of an inner God, we cannot find the open road or path. There is a story of the ancient gods searching for a suitable place in which to hide the power of this universe (God). They could not seem to find such a place at first until finally, one of the gods thought to hide the power inside a human being. No one would ever look for it there! This is sad, but true. God, as Light, truly resides within us and we in Him. What greater power could we have?

Find the truth; know that you are truly a being of light. Walk in the light; deliberately feel that you are stepping into this energy and you will sense a feeling of freedom. You are no longer bound by physical needs or seeming limitations because the recognition and *acceptance* of this light has set you free. Being a spiritual person means living the truth as you see it; applying that truth. So, radiate this light throughout your entire being and out to others. By so doing, you will experience yourself as a free spirit in God's eternal universe!

The prayer that follows on page 24 is from Jim Goure. It is a wonderful example of how to understand and express the spiritual, universal Light:

The Seven Step Effective Prayer
(from the United Research Light Center, Black Mountain, NC)

1. I release all of my past to the Light—fears, death, money, sex, human relationships, the future and all negatives.
2. I am a Light Being.
3. I radiate the Light from my Light Center throughout my whole being.
4. I radiate the Light from my Light Center to everyone.
5. I radiate the Light from my Light Center to everything.
6. I am in a bubble of Light. Only Light can come to me and only Light can be here.
7. Thank you, God, for everyone, for everything and for me.

CHAPTER 4

DARKNESS
AND LIGHT

There are numerous ways to understand this mysterious element called Light. Likewise, there are
many aspects to that which we call darkness.
Darkness is not always negative. There are many
positive aspects to darkness; it may give a feeling
of warmth and quietness; it symbolizes the birthing
of a new idea. All seeds germinate in the dark, in
the protection of the night, being free of the noise
and confusion of the outer world. However, the
seed in the ground is not truly in darkness; it is
being protected from physical daylight and electrical energies. It is filled with an inner light that is
necessary for its growth, as light is not merely light
per se, but is LIFE itself.

We need to escape at times from our immediate and material surroundings to find the "peace of
God, which passeth all understanding" (Philippians

4:7). Often, just sitting outside alone on a dark
night can fill us with a feeling of mystique, and can
lift our consciousness into a more ethereal level.
So, darkness offers a positive and supportive side
to life. It indicates the period of time when the
earth rests. However, shutting off the world and
staying in darkness should not be a constant experience. We must *always* return to the light.

There are many different ways of comprehend-
ing darkness. Darkness erases light, but are there
not times when we need to turn off the light and go
within, into the physical hiding place where we can
be alone? We have not turned off the Inner Light,
because we go to be alone. We have merely
"escaped" into quietness, into a "nothingness," so
we may become more aware of the special light
that is at the center of our being; that light which
will guide us through the "negative" darkness (or
blindness) into deeper awareness. A new idea is
brewing. Our creative genius is trying to sprout. The
physically blind can sense this inner light and can
radiate it perhaps to a greater extent than can
those who "see." They may often be more open
and receptive to this Divine Light than those who
perceive physically, but are blind spiritually. As
Marguerite Radclyffe-Hall said in the song "The
Blind Ploughman," "God took away my sight that
my soul might see."

We all need a time of silence, we need to be
alone, while holding to that feeling of Oneness with
the Divine. The "sprouts" of our creativity must, in
fact, be in a hiding place before they can truly blossom forth. In order to grow new wings, the seeds

have been planted and must, before long, release the darkness and embrace the light. Otherwise, no growth is possible. Stagnation is the result if we remain too long in darkness.

When we are deprived of light, we get depressed. There is an extremely high suicide rate in Alaska and the Scandinavian countries, for prolonged periods of darkness undoubtedly cause deep depression. This presents a great challenge. When we are so enveloped in darkness, we must make a supreme effort to bring forth the light within—to feel and visualize it filling our being and surroundings. Full spectrum light, even though only physical, can bring an upliftment of spirit.

"Darkness," when it is used to represent negativity, is expressed by the fears we exhibit, by our succumbing to illness, when we become angry and frustrated. *That* is when we experience what St. John called the "dark night of the soul." If we live in a state of insecurity and emotional trauma, we are living in darkness. It can become a positive experience when we recognize the negatives as challenges and opportunities for spiritual growth. The darkness of our negative emotions and experiences could be analogous to a huge mirror by which we may learn to look at ourselves honestly and constructively. It is, in a sense, turning on the light for us to step out of the night into daylight which brings a learning perspective to our actions, thoughts, and feelings. Sometimes, looking into the past can put us into a state of darkness. However, by focusing the light on the past, it can change our *perception* of it. Facts remain facts, but by viewing past events in the light, it is as though a different colored lamp had been turned on and suddenly the entire picture changes. We are more detached, we have stepped aside to "look," and the hurts and unhappiness have become transformed into positive steps of learning. (Please refer to the Seven Step Prayer in chapter 3, page 23.)

Since our thoughts direct energy waves, they are forming patterns and reconstructing atoms— either for positive creations or for destruction. This all depends on one's level of consciousness. We can send forth (and we do) thought forms that are either healing or of a negative nature. There are no in-betweens. "When a boulder is rolled away from a cave, the light filters in. It's as though there had never been any darkness. The same is true when we shine a light in the dark corners of our inner lives."[1] Not only in our lives, but in those of others also.

So, darkness wears many hats. It *can* be purposeful. In meditation, for instance, we close our eyes to shut out the light that we may then "see." We tune in to vibrations beyond the physical, and to be more receptive to Masters on the higher planes, we often need to remove ourselves temporarily from the lower, materialistic world. Being enfolded in this quietness and peace gives us strength and a deeper awareness of our own spirituality. We feel the touch of our spirit guides, and we know we are in the Presence of the One. This expe-

---

[1] Louise P. Hauck, *Beyond Boundaries* (Nevada City, CA: Blue Dolphin, 1992), p. 66.

rience, however, does not in any way imply that being in the "outer" light prohibits any "inner" seeing. Meditating in the "dark" is merely a step upward in growth. As the purpose of darkness is but temporary, yet necessary on this plane of life, then light and darkness may be thought of as opposing vibrations, but in reality they work together. We cannot speak of heat without considering its opposite—cold; there is no light without darkness. "If there were no good, we would never be able to conceive of evil."[2] The idea and necessity of opposites originated from the Chinese symbol of Yin-Yang, indicating that opposites must, and do, intertwine with each other.

"Absolute light and absolute darkness are opposites that come together to create a perfect unity."[3] A paradox it may seem, but in reality, darkness can never eradicate light, as light is life, itself. It has been noted by scientists that in each tiny cell in our bodies, there is an infinitesimal spark of light. When the cell dies, the spark dies also. However, light is still in the body. When a lightbulb in the room dies out, it may be dark, but the true light is still there. It is only our *perception* of darkness that impresses us with the loss of light, and the two elements compliment each other. They are two sides of the same coin. Eventually, we will not even see darkness as a negative, but will understand it as a lesson—pointing out a stepping stone

---

[2] Richard Morris, *Light: From Genesis to Modern Physics* (New York: Macmillan, 1979), p. 4.

[3] Harvey Humann, *The Many Faces of Angels* (Marina del Rey, CA: DeVorss, 1986), p. 75.

to growth. Therefore, we will comprehend it as light. "When mind has only light, it knows only light. . . . Each one you see in light brings your light closer to your awareness."[4]

> It is important to remember that miracles and vision necessarily go together . . . the miracle is always there. . . . You will see them in the light; you will not see them in the dark.[5]

> "The light of the body is the eye: if therefore thine eye be single, thy whole body shall be full of light. But if thine eye be evil, thy whole body shall be full of darkness. If therefore the light that is in thee be darkness, how great is that darkness" (Matthew 6:22-23).

---

[4] Barbara Fundisen, *Course in Miracles Concordance* (Farmingdale, NY: Coleman Graphics, 1983), p. 286.
[5] Foundation For Inner Peace, *A Course in Miracles*, p. 154.

CHAPTER 5

THE LIGHT
OF ANGELS

The word "angel" comes from the Greek "angelos," meaning messenger—or a Being of celestial realms. We call angels Messengers of Light, helpers and guardians to human beings. According to Geoffrey Hodson, angels are formed out of Divine Light manifesting in flaring energies and vibrant colors. They are aerial bodies, not just pure thought. They have been described as being like "lightning dressed in snow." "The astral bodies of angels and archangels are fields of light from which they are able to project temporary appearances."[1] The wings that are portrayed so often by artists are not exactly part of their light bodies, and yet, as described by Flower Newhouse (a Christian Mystic), the high vibrations

---

[1] Manly P. Hall, *The Blessed Angels* (Los Angeles: Philosophical Research Press, 1980), p. 45.

of their light energies produce this effect which gives the appearance of wings.

The angelic kingdom has long been a mystery to many. Some say that angels are merely good thoughts; others say that they are a beautiful fantasy, and yet, there are many who testify to having seen and communed with them. There are many biblical references to angel visitations, and there are at least three hundred recorded instances of such experiences. Many of our poets, musicians, and artists report seeing angelic beings as well as seeing little nature spirits. There was a report during World War II of a group of soldiers having seen at one time an "army of angels" surrounding the British troops.

According to some authorities, angels were not created in the beginning, as we were. They followed the creation of the first people, but once created, they may live thousands and thousands of years and may be immortal. The belief in the existence of the angelic kingdom has been around for thousands of years, and some archaeologists found, in a city 4000 years old, an engraving on a stone that was very similar to an angel form as we know it.

Just where are the angels? What is their purpose and how do they relate to us?

First, angels are on their own particular path of evolution; they are not a part of the human path, nor do humans become angels. However, there is a symbiotic relationship and communication between the angelic kingdom and mankind, and these two paths may be considered parallel in evolving to the Godhead. Angels can, and do, materialize before us when needed, but their presence also can be felt without a physical "seeing." They can be localized, but cannot be in more than one place at the same time. This differs from the great Masters who, because of their heightened spiritual consciousness, can manifest in more than one place at the same time.

It is thought by some that all music originates from the songs of angels. There are angels of music, art, healing, prayer, and many others; also guardian angels, not only for humans, but for animals and plants as well. There is a purpose for them all and they follow the will of God; they do not have free will as do humans.

Nature spirits from the devic kingdom all have a close relationship with the angelic kingdom. The word *deva* is a Sanskrit word meaning the "shining ones," and indicates other life forms within nature itself. There are many who believe in nature spirits. Two very special people who wrote about this subject from their own understanding and observations are Geoffrey Hodson, a theosophist, who wrote *Fairies at Work and at Play*, and Flower Newhouse, a Christian mystic who wrote *The Kingdom of the Shining Ones*.

Just as angels are on a different plane than humans, so are many other forms of life—air and water spirits, for example. There are undoubtedly many varied vibrational levels of life which may be expressed within different beings. Differences in vibrational levels would also imply a variation of etheric matter around our Earth which could make possible the variety of life forms. The light is with these tiny water, fire, and air beings and has been observed by people who have inner vision.

The question may be asked, "Why do we need the angels, the nature spirits, the teachers?" God chose to manifest in many diverse ways to express LIFE. For example, there are many different kinds of flowers, trees, lush forests; they all radiate beauty and a certain level of light energy. Perhaps this manifests the unlimitedness of the Creator. Not only in nature do we see so many differences, but also in mankind; we are made up of various races, cultures, life-expressions. Not only on this earth plane, but throughout the cosmos, the universal ethers are teeming with life and light. We may use the term "differences," yet all is One and everything, everywhere has but *one* root cause—the Universal, Spiritually Omniscient Being.

The awareness of the existence of angels is becoming much more prevalent as the earth and its inhabitants approach a new dimension—a higher level of consciousness. Many contacts are coming forth as we become more receptive and more open to the light. Angels appear in the light—their auras make them visible. Their light is so brilliant that it raises our vibratory level so we can see these beautiful life forms. Their purpose is to guide and help us. The luminescence they radiate is a part of Divine Light, and brings energy and truth to those who accept in humility and trust.

We know that our guardian angels and all other angelic beings are a reality and a necessary part of God's limitless (unimaginable?) universe. They aid us on this plane and even act as guides for those having "near death experiences." They help others who are actually stepping over from this plane to the next phase of life. As we allow our own inner light to grow, we shall have greater awareness of the angelic light energies.

No matter how we may perceive the angels personally, they have become symbols of ultimate beauty, light, perfection, and love. They add a spiritual dimension that transcends all religious doctrines. May the Light of the Angels shine upon you!

CHAPTER 6

HOW DO WE USE LIGHT ENERGIES?

We know the light is here; it is within us, but what are we doing with it? How do we use it for ourselves and for others? "We have all the light we need, we just need to put it into practice."[1]

Light can open so many doors for us. It enables us to "see" into other galaxies, to see beyond the veil into greater spiritual dimensions and to see the truth within outer appearances. The application of light allows us to delve deeper into life's mysteries. Native Americans, for example, believe that, as they worship the Great White Spirit, the veil will be removed, letting them see beyond the horizon of the physical plane.

How do you feel when you walk into a dimly lit room? And how do you feel when a bright light is

---

[1] Arthur Zajonc, *Catching the Light* (New York: Bantam, 1993), p. 1.

suddenly turned on, making the entire room cheer-
ful and energizing? By turning on the light in the
darkness, we are enabled to see our surroundings,
to understand what is before us—people, conditions, and so forth. Then, by "turning on" the light
within, we gain a deeper comprehension of what
the outer symbols represent to us. The inner light
directs our thinking, our knowing. The true light
can be our teacher, our guide, our healer, if we
allow it.

When we are looking for direction or for a solution to a problem, we need to shut off the world
momentarily. We need to be still and visualize the
light from the One flowing freely into our entire
being, filling our awareness with wisdom and
knowledge. We do not receive this if we are putting
up blocks of frustration, anger, or doubt. But, by
truly detaching, if only for a moment, we become
receptive to our good.

The light is here for all of us to use, but how do
we use this energy of which we are a part? We must
first establish ourselves in this light, *knowing* that
we are in the light and are an integral part of this
one and only spiritual light. As we begin to *feel* and
see ourselves filled with these vibrations, then we
know we can stand tall; we can enjoy health; we
can be at peace and we can begin to heal and
serve others. We must learn to apply these energies
even on the most mundane levels knowing that the
light can guide and direct us in the most seemingly
insignificant things, and we must not hesitate to
apply it in everyday matters. Changes can be
brought about in our lives when we attain a deeper

understanding of the guidance that light can bring us, once we open ourselves to it with sincere acceptance. Light *can* transform us. It can also be used for healing.

Someone we know may have a terminal illness or may be undergoing extreme mental and emotional problems. Our task, or opportunity, would be to see the individual in this light by projecting a circle of healing light around this person. By visualizing, we create. As we know that this super energy has the power to transmute, cleanse, and heal, we can then project it with our thoughts. The objective is to direct this healing light to the root cause of the problem, rather than merely healing the symptoms, so that a true healing may take place.

Healing light has the power to dispel any attack of hate, anger, or violence. If we understand and have faith in the tremendous spiritual energy in these vibrations, we can use them constructively. We meet all kinds of challenges in life. Are we not confronted by these challenges to help us in our own spiritual growth? Light—synonymous with love—is a protective shield if we believe it and apply it. By truly experiencing and applying these great vibrational energies, we can conquer evil. Evil can never be overcome by evil, but can be affected and changed by working with the positive energy of light.

Let us consider the direct use of physical light and the light of the sun, each of which, of course, is an integral part of Divine Light. In reality, there is no separation in any of our universal vibrations and energy. There are numerous techniques we can use to apply spiritual light.

The use of artificial light bulbs focused on a person can be healing if there is depression, fear, insecurity, or any similar condition. Full spectrum light can duplicate pure sunlight as no rays are then filtered out. We must recognize the importance of pure light not only for physical healing, but for mental and emotional balancing as well. During the second century, Greek and Roman doctors pre-scribed the necessity of exposing oneself to direct sunlight for the healing of depression. "Before World War II, most hospitals were built with a solari-um or sun room. The 'light bath' was popular in Europe; 'helio-therapy', it was called, after Helios, the Greek god of the sun."[2]

When we take the initiative to change ourselves and *really* walk in the light, we can make a tremen-dous difference in the world around us. Not that we directly change others, but by our own positive radiations of love and light, others will behold this light which banishes darkness. "And I, if I be lifted up from the earth, will draw all men unto me" (John 12:32).

Sometimes we feel that the path of light is a hard one to follow. Actually, it should be the easi-est way. There will, however, come a time when you will walk every day knowing that you are truly a part of that Divine Light, that you *are* the light, and it is with you constantly. You will not have to make a conscious effort to be in the light; you will just

---

[2] Lee Kremis More, *Poughkeepsie Journal* (Dec. 1994): 1D.

know that you are always with, in and of the light. The Great Master has told us that we are the light of the world. Believe it.

We can confront any predicament with "tools" of compassion, wisdom, and the application of light energy, rather than with anger and a desire for retaliation. Violence need not be, nor *can* it be the answer to confronting evil. If we should experience a negative attack from someone, we should immediately project a bubble of light around the individual and around ourselves, *knowing* that this energy has the power to immediately transform the person and protect us. As we eliminate fear and hate, we are then recipients and dispensers of healing, support, and unconditional love. Bathe the negativity with love.

Let us consider world situations. First, we are taught to love one another, to bless those who persecute us. Also, we are told not to kill, except, as the "world" would direct us—when defending ourselves or our country?! Do we listen to a Higher Guidance? If so, then we learn of a higher way of "defense" and protection. It is possible and imperative that we choose the high road and work with our spiritual understanding. We can then apply the power and strength of the light/love energies to dispel adverse conditions, rather than fighting to kill. However, to bring the world into consciousness of peace and light can only start with the individual. Changes can and will develop as they start from the light of a single divine candle within the human being. "Crime will never be wiped out until the day people decide to use light."[3] If we are truly radiating light, we are also radiating love, and this is the greatest healing power with which we are endowed.

Since light is a symbol of wisdom and knowledge, how do we bring others into this state of awareness? It is said that "Diogenes, the great Greek sage, always carried a lamp as the symbol of the divine light or the light of the spirit in man. He used to go from house to house and awaken all the people with that light."[4] This, of course, is symbolic of our need (desire) to share this light of understanding and wisdom with all mankind. If we let the light that is within shine forth in our daily lives, it will be observed and received by others. There are many whose light shines forth so brilliantly that no words or teachings are necessary. The feeling is there; the energy is there, and just being in the presence of such a one is sufficient to change another's life. The responsibility is great—to develop our own inner light to such an extent that we may serve others by trying to aid them in their awakening.

Another path on our application of the light is to allow it to raise our consciousness to a level where the Illumined Masters on the inner planes may be drawn by the light and therefore, a needed contact will be made with our guides, helpers, and teachers. The light draws them to us, but also per-

---

[3] Omraam Mikhael Aivanhov, *Life Is A Living Spirit* (Los Angeles: Prosveta, 1984), p. 50.

[4] Swami Bodhananda, *Lectures on Vedanta Philosophy* (New Rochele, NY: Knickerbocker Press, 1928), p. 149.

mits us to enter a higher rate of vibration where we may learn and experience ever more on our now-illuminated spiritual path.

To find meaning in life, we must first "turn on the switch." However, before we can feel its full intensity, we must understand this "twin" quality of love. "In fact, if you are to obtain this light, you must understand the importance of the questions of love. When you really know how to understand love, how to manifest it and how to let it flow through you, you will become luminous."[5]

Once we do become filled with this wonderfully divine energy which is life itself, then the meaning of our life becomes visible to us; we no longer have doubts and fears. We now see the light on the path and we know that the light/love vibrations will direct us as we allow ourselves to be open and receptive.

In summarizing the uses and meaning of light, the following ways can be used to project this energy:

1. We must fill our meditation time completely with light.
2. Surround all negativity on the planet in a bubble of the pure, white light of Spirit.
3. Send light for healing by "seeing" the dis-eased person fully enveloped by the light rather than looking at the imbalance.

---

[5] Omraam Mikhael Aivanhov, *Light Is A Living Spirit,* p. 60.

4. Use the understanding power of light to transmute past experiences of discord and hurt into positive energy.
5. Allow the light to give us direction and guidance on our path. This can be realized only by "letting go" and giving our complete attention to this light.
6. Let the light fill us completely with a sense of Oneness with the great Divine Essence over all.

As we fill areas of "seeming" negativity with the light, we begin to comprehend these areas differently. Light reveals the truth that there is a purpose and plan in all things. There are no "accidents." As we open ourselves to the revelations of the light, we begin to perceive more of truth, and our understanding of life deepens as we continue to turn the switch a bit higher and higher. So, light your candle and keep it glowing!

CHAPTER 7

SCIENTIFIC ASPECTS OF LIGHT

As we begin to explore the scientific side of light, let us remember that there is a continuous connection between both physical and spiritual light. We consider the scientific side to be an electromagnetic radiation with a qualitative intensity of brightness. There are many divisions of light, the laser being a very important one which is used in many healing treatments. The laser light is made up of atoms having an unusual level of energy. The laser itself may be thought of as a hollow tube resembling an organ pipe, which is tuned to a specific wave length of emitted photons. This coherent light—all portions of optical wave fronts vibrating in unison—is used today in many surgical procedures, especially for eye surgery. The lasers are also used for such purposes as welding, cutting, and drilling, and in labs for fusion research and spectrographic analysis. The lasers are also now very important in the telecommunication and music industries.

There have been many differences in the understanding of light rays, particles and waves, and their various uses. Interested readers may want to explore the study of optics, which refers to all phenomena related to light. For example, geometric optics deals with reflection, refraction and the formation of images by optical instruments; physical optics is a study of optical phenomena in regards to the wave nature of light; and quantum optics deals with the particle nature of light, as in the photoelectric effect. This study of optics began around 300 B.C. Many scientists have explored this field, such as Isaac Newton, who published his book *Optics* in 1704. Newton performed many original optical tests by which he learned that white light can be broken into colors by use of a prism, and it can also be re-combined with a second prism.

•   •   •

There are many concerns regarding exposure to ultraviolet light; many feel they must protect themselves from sunlight. While it is true that large amounts of ultraviolet light can be harmful, there are many indications that it can stimulate the immune system and can be a strong nutrient for the body. A certain amount of sunlight is necessary for a healthy life.

According to Dr. Jacob Liberman in *Light: Medicine of the Future*, "Light traveling through the eyes directly affects the nutrients in the blood, allowing them to be completely absorbed by the body as usable food."[1] By protecting ourselves with sunglasses, we are blocking the healing qualities of ultraviolet light. According to Liberman there are many benefits of ultraviolet light, such as lowering blood pressure, increasing efficiency of the heart, reducing cholesterol, assisting in weight control, increasing the level of sex hormones, and effectively treating many other diseases or conditions. It is indeed sad to realize that so many people spend many years of their lives under artificial lighting, yet so many light bulbs are completely free of ultraviolet light.

This brief overview of the physical concepts related to light opens up unlimited possibilities for relating the scientific to the metaphysical understanding of light. There is yet much to discover and learn in the field of physics, but the growth of knowledge will lead humanity into a deeper understanding of the integration of the physical light with the philosophical/spiritual light, that which guides, energizes, and gives meaning to life.

---

[1] Dr. Jacob Liberman, *Light: Medicine of the Future* (Santa Fe: Bear & Co., 1991), p. 158.

CHAPTER 8

RELIGIOUS LIGHT

There are many ways to acknowledge the light we explore in this book. In this chapter, I present a very brief overview of light used in different religions—from celebrating the light, to understanding what it symbolizes for humanity. All religions and all cultures celebrate this light that modern people seem to have lost. We shall look at examples from the Jewish tradition, the Baha'i, the Buddhist, Hindu, Christian, and Native Americans. This overview is not intended to be complete; I am just presenting various concepts so readers can see that the tradition of "light" is very old.

Lighting a candle brings us a symbol—a part of the Divine Light that illuminates the world. When candles are lighted for Shabbat and for the Holidays celebrated in the Jewish tradition, hearts are filled with joy.

There is a 3700-year old tradition among the Jewish women to welcome the Sabbath Queen by lighting the candles. It is considered the Mitzvah that lights the divine spark in every Jew. This lighting of candles brings light to the world to dispel darkness. The women and girls of Jewish faith are encouraged to project this holy light to the earth so that its illumination will cleanse and enlighten the planet.

The Jewish holidays are the dedicated times for their candle-lighting rites. This brings the joy of pronouncing the Bracha (blessing) which they know brings the love and approval of "G-d." Jewish girls develop the strength of their own inner light by participating in these ceremonies. They learn that the inner light becomes a beacon to guide them throughout their lives. They know that these candle-lighting sacraments bring incredible energy to their envisioning of a glorious future and universal peace.

The Light is within us. As King Solomon said, "The Soul of man is the candle of G-d." The word for light in Hebrew is "Or," also meaning "secret." These two words have a numerical relationship; so "He who has the light has the secret."

Light is an explanation of how godliness is found in the world. God is in all places at the same time and His Essence never changes. As expressed in Judaism, the sun shines everywhere. Sunlight can fill a room and can also fill a "broken vessel." This symbology seems to indicate that Divine Light is within everything and everyone, even in those who are out of balance and unaware. The pertinent point of this universal light, however, is—how do we perceive it and how do we utilize it?

"Chabad," meaning wisdom, understanding, and knowledge pertains to the Masters who are leaders of the Chassidic movement. They help bring unity between a person and G-d; to do a kindness and to apply everything in life for service to G-d. On a physical level we might understand the purpose of some Chassidic members who went to many homes, bringing lamps for people to light their rooms. This helped to create a gathering, and a sharing of the light. Might this not be considered symbolic of the joining of one another in their search for the light of wisdom and understanding?

Light is the essence of the God-created world. It is light that gives energy for world to exist, but if this light isn't connected with the source, there can be no existence. Light allows us to recognize what is already around us. For example, if we walk into a darkened room where there is an obstacle which cannot be seen, then we may be harmed. However, if we turn on the light, we are no longer in the darkness, and we are able to see the problem and find a solution for it. We do not always appreciate the light until we find ourselves in the darkness.

The Judaic explanation of Creation is that G-d sent *only one* infinitesimal spark of His Light to remove the void, as creation could not endure the intensity of the *totality* of the Divine Light. As with the extreme brightness of sunlight, our physical eyes cannot tolerate too great a vibration. Likewise, our spiritual Self has not yet arrived at a high enough consciousness to accept the ALLness or fullness of the light and energy of the Divine Creator. However, just a small drop of light can represent G-d to us, *depending on our receptivity.*

"Just as a candle requires lighting before it can perform its function, our souls must be kindled before they can brighten up our lives and illuminate the lives of others in turn. We must all become "lamplighters" igniting the sparks that lie dormant in one another's hearts."[1]

•   •   •

According to the Baha'is, those who are in a high state of spiritual consciousness and receptivity to truth are in the "Day of Reckoning," filled with light of true understanding, and are open to great divine gifts. When people allow the light of truth to guide them, peace and understanding are theirs. God is our Light in the heavens and on Earth. If we are not on the divine path, we are considered to be guilty of many negatives. God is within all people and all things visible and invisible, but those who are without the light are unable to perceive this.

For the Baha'i's, Light shines forth on the Illumined Ones even though they may live in physical poverty. Those "in the light" do not recognize poverty or helplessness as such, since they are ever aware of spiritual riches and divine glory. The illumined teachers and prophets are recognized as

---

[1] Simcha Gottlieb, *Let There Be Light* (New York: Merkos Linyonei Chinuch, 1987), jacket copy.

"mirrors that truly and faithfully reflect the light of God."[2]

Light is knowledge, but we close the door to light when we persist in negative actions and thoughts, for "backbiting quencheth the light of the heart and extinguisheth the life of the soul."[3] Being in and of the light brings one to a greater awareness of truth. As we follow its guidance, it becomes a deterrent of evil doing. This inextinguishable Divine Light is termed "Urvatu'l-Va<u>th</u>ga."[4]

God's purpose in sending prophets and illumined ones is to guide humanity toward the light, for the unity of all mankind. The Baha'is compare the variety of prophets in different ages to the Moon that reflects radiant light to the Earth, "though every time it appeareth, it revealeth a fresh measure of its brightness, yet its inherent splendor can never diminish nor can its light suffer extinction."[5] An analogy is made between the daily rising of the sun and the light of Divine Revelation as it reaches mankind according to the individual's capacity or receptivity to spiritual consciousness and the ability to grow to an increasing intensity of light. This light envelops our entire creation.

Illumination and the "light of unity" will come to those who would hear the words and accept the

---

[2] Baha'u'llah, *The Book of Certitude* (Wilmette, IL: Baha'i Publishing Trust, 1931), p. 142.
[3] Baha'u'llah, *The Book of Certitude*, p. 193.
[4] Baha'u'llah, *Kitab-I-IQuan* (Wilmette, IL: The Baha'i Publishing Trust, 1993), p. 205.
[5] Baha'u'llah, *Gleanings From the Writings of Baha'u'llah* (Wilmette, IL: The Baha'i Publishing Trust, 1952), p. 79.

truth. The entire Earth will be uplifted, and the power of this "light of unity," when fully expressed, will illuminate the whole planet. According to Baha'u'llah, the purpose of God in revealing himself to mankind "is to lay bare those gems that lie hidden within the mine of their true and inmost selves."[6]

Other aspects of light, according to the Baha'is, are tolerance and righteousness, termed "luminaries" or two lights which can clear the darkness. Baha'u'llah teaches that religion is a radiant light which can protect humanity. When the light is hidden from mankind, peace and tranquillity cease. It is "hidden" only when our earthly inhabitants fail to respect and regard religion as Divine Light. "The world's horizon is resplendent with the light of the Most Great Luminary, yet the generality of mankind sees it not."[7]

• • •

Buddhists are familiar with the light that we speak of as well. The Buddha, who appeared on this plane in the fifth century, B.C., represents Enlightenment. He continued the early Aryan tradition of the search for enlightenment, spiritual liberation, and Nirvana. Sākyamuni, founder of Buddhism, attained enlightenment, was released from the bondage of ignorance (Avijja), and achieved the perfect wisdom. There are many sets of opposite ideas expressed in Buddhist Scripture: light and darkness, wisdom and ignorance, purity and impurity, samsāra and nirvana.

---

[6] *Gleanings From the Writings of Baha'u'llah*, p. 287.
[7] Ibid., p. 236.

Symbols, as expressed in some of the Buddha's teachings, reflect the image of light and darkness:

> The sun shines by day;
> The moon shines by night;
> The warrior shines in armour;
> The Brahmin shines in meditation,
> But the Buddha shines the whole day and
>   night by his glory.[8]

Buddhist teachings recommend the acquisition of virtuous qualities, such as wisdom, purity, lovingkindness, learning, intelligence, and righteousness. The Lokuttara School of early Buddhism describes the Buddha as having the unlimited splendor and unlimited longevity that are attributed to a divinity in the West. The Buddha possessed the six supernatural powers; i.e., the heavenly eye, heavenly ear, telepathy, remembering one's previous existence, transformation into various forms, and the elimination of defilements. People who followed the Buddha's path also sought to develop these qualities.

We learn that the Buddha possessed the thirty-two attributes of a superman. One of these mentions his great light, which gave great illumination around his entire body. It was also stated in the Sukhāvati-vyaha Sūtra that Amitabha Buddha has a halo on his head which is similar in size to the 1,000,000,000 world systems, and in it there are

---

[8] Buddha, *The Dhammapada*, trans. U. Dhammajoti (Benares, India: The Maha-Bodhi Society, 1943), No. 387.

one hundred thousand billion Buddhas who are as numerous as the sands of the Ganges River in India.

Many Buddhists believe that one can become an adept without a teacher, as we all have that Inner Light which should, of itself, teach us truth, wisdom, and spirituality. Each one, then, moves and grows according to the awareness of that light within. Monks today are instructed to "follow a regimen Buddha set for his disciples 2500 years ago— 'Be a light unto yourself, a refuge unto yourself.'"[10]

On the popular level of religious practices, the offering of incense sticks, oil lamps, and flowers at Buddhist shrines and temples is a normal practice among Buddhists everywhere. On special occasions, such as on the day of his attainment of Buddhahood, or that of his reaching the final nirvana, a festival of light is held. This festival is a national holiday. These festivals celebrate the fact that the wisdom of the Buddha enlightens the world of darkness and ignorance, and thereby all sentient beings will be enabled to cross over the ocean of sufferings.

The 19th-century Buddhist priest, Musō Kokushi, mentioned the ancients who feel that "every sentient being possesses a spiritual light drawn from 'the samadhi of the Storehouse of the Great Light.' The 'miracle-light' of all the Buddhas is drawn from this same source.'"[11] This original

[10] Joseph M. Kitagawa, "The Eightfold Path," in *Great Religions of the World* ed. Gilbert M. Grosvenor (Washington, DC: National Geographic Society, 1971), p. 120.
[11] Arthur Zajonc, *Catching the Light* (New York: Bantam, 1993), pp. 158-159.

source of light is the essence of spirituality, and of our inner knowing. Many people are unaware of this, however, and see *only* the physical light.

•   •   •

Native Americans also celebrate Light. The Cherokees believe that the Sun is the life giver— the father—and the Earth is the mother. They feel there are as many ways to reach the source of this life as there are people on Earth. Everyone must find their own path to this "life-giver." They pray to the Sun. The Spirit of the East is as golden as the Rising Sun and is called Enlightenment of Illumination, for it frees them from the darkness of ignorance.

When Hopis need guidance, they "open the door" at the top of their heads to receive the light which gives the needed direction. One of the sacred names of the Lakota tribe (also known as the Sioux) is Chalíse, meaning "a chalice overflowing with light." This tribe has a great awareness of light—its various meanings and many usages. They often speak of the Masters as spreading their teachings in a "spiral of light." The Lakotas are so attuned to Nature that they take time to "see" spirit in rocks, trees, the sky, and in all forms of life. They believe in the Oneness of life and they worship the sky, the sun, and the rainbow (which they term the "bridge of light"). "The bridge into a new time must be a bridge of light—all colors, all races. All Our Relations must be included in that bridge for the rainbow to form and to arch across the chasm."[12] Many rituals were developed which caused light and colors to appear in many ways and parts of nature. One of their Great Ones (referred to as Grandma) of their tribe was called the "Woman Who Knows Everything." She was a tiny, frail and wizened woman who "began to shine with golden light and unfolded out of herself into a radiant woman of light."[13] She was able to radiate light forth whenever it was needed, in a positive and constructive way, by surrounding someone, or a place, with it. "Miracles are natural when we allow the love and light of the Great Spirit and Mother Earth to shine forth unrestricted from our hearts . . ."[14]

The Moon's cycles also have significance for Native Americans. They call the Moon, Grandmother Moon. They spend time in the moonlight where there are no artificial lights and get in rhythm with the Moon's waxing and waning. (Think of yourselves when you feel the light is waning; remember, the *fullness* of its light is ever there and will always return.) They feel the Moon encourages one to rest, to be quiet and to go within. "My elders say that if one in ten thousand two-leggeds stands in the light, then the light comes for all of us."[15]

This Sioux tribe puts great importance on peace and the Oneness of all life. They live very

---

[12] Brooke Medicine Eagle, *Buffalo Woman Comes Singing* (New York: Ballantine, 1991), p. 113.
[13] Ibid., p. 21.
[14] Ibid., p. 238.
[15] Ibid., p. 346.

close to Nature and feel a true relationship with Grandmother Moon, Mother Earth and the Great Spirit over everything. The light of wisdom is within them and they use it in service to others.

• • •

Light to the Christians is represented by the truth that was brought forth from Jesus the Christ. It was first manifested by the star that shone so brightly that special night; that starlight that led the Magi to the manger which was filled with a profusion of divine illumination. This was a lesson for mankind—to look up, to raise the consciousness that leads to the Path, and to travel in faith never doubting, but knowing that the light always shines, if we are willing to be open to such radiance.

The teachings of Christ illumine the way for Christians, as they begin to understand this great energy called light. Christ represented pure light, and He taught human beings that they are also of this same light; that humans are more than mere physical beings; they are of spirit. Christians believe that the Christ Light is within everyone and points the way to a higher and eternal life, once it is acknowledged and followed. The way is always open.

Jesus demonstrated the power of light and it shone through him wherever he went. The Christ Light is the light that "lighteth every man" and Christians know that this light is to be followed. The "I AM" represents this spark within and, as contact is made with it, joy, happiness and love, which is synonymous with light, fills the soul.

According to the New Testament, many miracles were performed by Christ, through the great light energy which permeated His being and radiated out to others. As Christianity developed, more and more Christians began to realize that this great power was within them also. "As thou hast believed so be it done unto thee" (Matthew 8:13). As the light of understanding grows, every cell in the body becomes infused with light and knowledge. Christ taught that the strength of this wonderful light energy can manifest at will to perform "miracles." We need to realize that this Christ Consciousness is here for everyone to receive. Miracles, so-called, should be recognized as the acknowledgment of the Divine Power which can initiate such happenings, and are available to all. It is always the individual's choice to accept and apply this Divine Light whenever and wherever needed.

Miraculous events are really the results of *seeing* perfection, knowing the truth that the light has revealed, that bring an upliftment to the spiritual consciousness. Wonderful healing can be manifested from Spirit, and there can be an awakening from darkness that will bring distinct changes in our lives.

Many Christians have accepted stories of Jesus being in India (refer to *The Aquarian Gospel of Jesus the Christ* by Levi) from his youth to age 30, where he sat with many masters. Many great experiences and teachings were had by all.

Great light shone as Jesus and these spiritual masters met and communed with the light of God.

There are many different interpretations of the Christian philosophy, but the most pertinent teachings reveal the meaning of light as it opens the way to truth, wisdom, the releasing of negativities and the opening of their belief that Jesus, who became the Christed One, can lead them on the upward path. The biblical studies of Christ have further helped Christians to discover the way to rise above one's "sins," to experience love and to look forward to life eternal.

● ● ●

Hinduism, one of the world's oldest religions, is the most traditional and dominant religion of India. The Bhagavad Gita, sometimes called the "Lord's Song," is the most widely known of Hindu scriptures. In addition to specific spiritual teachings, the Hindus "invented" the zero and a numerical system superior to others! Among other writings, beside the Gita, are the Vedas which were written down about 1500 B.C.

The Hindus believe that God made Himself known many times in the physical manifestations of different masters. Krishna is one who was the master of great light as mentioned in the Bhagavad Gita. He taught his disciple, Arjuna, the principle of Right Thought leading to Right Action, always with the understanding of detachment, the main thrust of his teachings. The inner teachings of the Gita have not been interpreted for students, as the light will bring the truth directly to them, at the right time. "When the pupil is ready, the master is there."[16] It is true that when we are ready we will be aware of the light that is already there to point the way.

Krishna represents the light of wisdom and the inner truths of Hinduism, and as his students studied his teachings, they became more aware of the existence of this light, not only as to what it revealed to them, but that it was life itself. Krishna also taught that the Real Self can never be killed; life is eternal. Many of the principles given by Krishna are comparable to those taught by Jesus. Both instructed their disciples to follow and worship the One Spirit that is within all.

The Hindu name for God is Brahman. In the Gita, three ways are given for one to reach Brahman. They are, work and doing good deeds, meditation, and faith in and devotion to the one God.

The teachings of the Gita emphasize that the spiritual person lives in periods of contemplation in union with Divinity, even though the physical body and mind are active and at work. The idea of unity with all forms of life from the One Universal Source, is expressed within the Hindu writings. They teach that all forms are interdependent and they understand a range of intelligence which can benefit all.

------

[16] Yogi Ramacharaka, *The Bhagavad Gita* (Chicago: Yogi Publishing Society, 1935), p. 60.

We learn of the many manifestations of light as we study different religions, cultures, and teachers from various faiths. Although they are all reaching for the one Divine Spirit, there are many diverse roads to take, and many interpretations to discover. We are all one, yet individualizations of the One. We each must find our own path to the light. Learning to look, and then to follow that "lighted path," will lead us to our own special Guru, Master, studies, and life experiences.

CHAPTER 9

LUMINARIES

Albert Schweitzer is considered one of our illumined ones; one who chose to come into this plane of life with a multitude of talents in order to serve mankind and to bring beauty and love into the world.

The light brightly shines through such an individual. We may not always call a genius a "light being," but it is this divine energy within that enables us to bring forth great abilities. It is light that creates and points the way.

Dr. Schweitzer walked many paths. He was a theologian, philosopher, musicologist, and medical missionary, with doctorate degrees in all fields. The guiding light was certainly within him and inspired him to follow his inner feelings. In his 30th year, he began to concentrate on one of his many paths— that of medical missionary—and devoted the rest of his life to working with the people of South Africa. His other talents were certainly a part of this particular phase, as having a background of philosophy and theology must have definitely added substance to his healing work. Being an organist was also part of his expertise which added to the beauty and high energy which radiated forth from him. His recitals, along with lecture tours, and the publication of many books all brought monetary support for the hospital where he was doing his life's work. Among the many books he wrote were J.S. Bach and The Quest of the Historical Jesus.

Light strikes us in many ways and we receive according to our level of consciousness. Obviously, Dr. Schweitzer's was a high level of spiritual awareness, for his light took him on many paths of sharing and service.

George Fox, a man of wisdom, was very aware of the Christ Light within every human being. He recognized it well within himself, and as a result felt the inner direction to preach and talk with many groups who were considered "seekers." His groups grew and were originally called "Children of Light." Later, a more simplified term, the "Inner Light," was used to express their faith. Eventually, George Fox organized the peace-directed group called the Quakers.

It is quite meaningful to give thought to their meetings which were, and hopefully still are, meetings of silence, interrupted only when an individual feels led and inspired to speak. Learning to be quiet and to remain in the silence long enough to hear and feel the inner guidance is, indeed, a blessing.

One of the greatest attributes of the Quakers—also known as the Religious Society of Friends—is their belief in peace. They refuse to fight or kill for defensive purposes. During the Vietnam War, Quakers who were in favor of ending the war picketed the Federal buildings. They choose to send forth light to their adversaries rather than to become violent. One of their goals is to help to improve communication and decision-making to aid in promoting peace rather that allowing disagreements to cause war. Their inner light also directs them to promote improved education.

George Fox originated the art of consensual decision-making and taught people how to wait in silence before contributing their thoughts and suggestions: "how to not speak until moved, how to wait for the voice of their inner light, and ultimately, how to wait on the Lord."[1]

Scott Peck, who wrote so highly of George Fox, must be in agreement with the Quaker view of non-killing, and spoke of Welshmen defending against invaders and attacks made by the Royal Air Force. He said, "But I worry about the glory so generally attributed to such activity, then and now,"[2] and, "I do not mean to imply that going off to battle is never the holy thing to do; only that we have seriously lost our wits when we think that there is something inherently holy about warfare."[3]

---

[1] M. Scott Peck, *In Search of Stones* (New York: Hyperion, 1995), p. 117.
[2] *In Search of Stones*, p. 81.
[3] *In Search of Stones*, p. 81-82.

Aiming for peace certainly follows the admonitions of Christ who taught us to love one another, to "turn the other cheek" and to bless those who persecute us. As these principles are believed and acted upon, so will the light expressed by George Fox shine forth.

Father Damien is another important light in our past. Joseph de Veuster was in Belgium in 1840, and from childhood on he knew he wanted to be ordained as a priest, so that he could eventually become a missionary. He adopted the name of Damien, the fourth-century physician-martyr.

Before his ordination, he went to the Sandwich Islands where he did a great deal of physical labor in order to build a church. He gradually gathered a stock of medical supplies so that he might be the physician for his flock. He apparently felt that a light had been guiding him ever since his childhood. This light kept leading him on, and without a single doubt, he knew what his mission in life was to be.

A leper colony had been established on the island of Molokai, and at age 33, Damien received permission to go there to work. The courage and faith required to undertake this dangerous and unhealthy situation must have been born of his awareness of the Christ Light within him—the light that would give him strength to help all those suffering from leprosy. This light would also support him in his lifelong gift of sacrifice and devotion. He gradually gained the confidence of these patients for he tried to improve their living conditions. Anyone who can devote an entire life to such a tremendous service must indeed be a Light Being!

Father Damien died sixteen years later, after having developed leprosy himself. The light must have shone forth when he announced that he had the disease. Not only do people of this caliber bring love and light to those with whom they are close, but it spreads in many directions, and helps others to search for their own light, that it may lift them, also.

Walt Whitman was another great being who felt the light, lived in it, and radiated it in his contacts with nature and people. He expressed it as well in "Leaves of Grass."

People around Whitman experienced an exalted state after being in his presence; he changed many people's lives. There was a magnetism about him that reached out to others. The light was there. It was expressed in his friendliness, and in his close contact with all forms of Nature. Children felt his light and responded to him in a very positive way. He apparently released the many negatives that most people are prone to allow to enter their lives.

Whitman wrote in a very impromptu way and some of his earlier writings seemed to be of no great value. However, he had a great experience. He received illumination very unexpectedly one morning, and this experience, he felt, took complete hold of him. From then on, he felt he was a new person, and became so inspired that he felt an upliftment and his words became filled with light. Having become so receptive to this great flooding of inner light, he was led to an ever greater belief in eternal life, and had no fear of death.

For over twenty years, Whitman felt he was being guided by a great supernatural illumination. He acknowledged this spiritual upliftment and credited it to the Supreme Being in whom he had an unwavering belief.

As we grow on the ladder of spiritual awareness and lift the consciousness higher and higher, we reach a point where we appreciate the beauty of the simplicities in life. Walt Whitman lived the simple life and saw beauty and light within all phases of light; "the simple and commonplace with him included the ideal and the spiritual."[4]

One flash of spiritual light can give us Divine Awareness for an entire lifetime, and produces the progression from self-consciousness to Self-Consciousness, and so it was with Walt Whitman. Being receptive to and aware of all life is assurance that all things work together for good, once we allow the door to open.

Dag Hammarskjold, born in 1905 in Sweden, was truly a man of the light. He devoted his life to working for our world. He was a most charming and good=natured individual, but he was also very humble, yet strong in his convictions, leadership, and in the art of diplomacy.

As a boy, he developed a deep sense of "personal religion" which lighted his way throughout all his many international contacts, decision-making tasks and lectures. His philosophy was to be true to one's inner convictions; not to deny them for the

---

[4] Richard Maurice Bucke, M.D., *Cosmic Consciousness* (New York: E. P. Dutton, 1969), p. 218.

sake of peace. He was quite an exceptional diplomat. Throughout his life, Hammarskjold treated everyone with respect, and believed that individuals can and do make a difference. In 1953 he was made Secretary-General of the United Nations. He was soon recognized as an exceptional leader and communicator. He never tried to be dramatic when giving speeches, and while his speeches seemed unclear to some, he tried to emphasize that words should be and can be a substitute for weapons in establishing peace.

His work took him to many countries and he had numerous consultations with international leaders. He accomplished a great deal in enlarging the power and influence of the UN, and was considered one of the greatest leaders of this century.

Although the majority of his time was spent working with the UN, he had many other interests, one being art, which he often discussed professionally. An interesting note is that at one of the many meetings he attended, he suddenly felt he needed a break. He rushed out, went into one of the areas at the UN where art was displayed, gazed for a time at an abstract painting, then returned to the meeting, refreshed and relaxed. Do we not often need to "take a break" in the midst of business and concentration, and let the light of beauty uplift and quiet us?

One of Hammarskjold's trips took him to Nepal where he visited the Himalayas and a Buddhist Shrine. He took pictures of this and wrote an article about it, which was later published in the National Geographic.

To summarize Hammarskjold's philosophy: "Never look down to test the ground before taking the next step: only he who keeps his eye fixed on the far horizon will find his right road. . . . Let the inner take precedence over the outer, the soul over the world wherever this may lead you."[5]

This great individual was called a "soldier of peace," which indeed he was. No one could work as Hammarskjold did, with his motivation and inspiration, and not be filled with light. Light works in many ways, but sometimes unbeknown to us. This wonderful "worker-for-peace" died in 1961, and was posthumously awarded the Nobel Peace Prize.

Paramahansa Yogananda was another, and quite recent, light being who allowed his inner awareness to receive divine direction for his life. His inner light was such that he was receptive to spirit masters and could see materializations of those in the ethereal bodies. He was be of great spiritual service to the world. He lived in India and later came to California because he was called by his spirit master to come. Here he established the Self-Realization Foundation. While there, among other things, he taught Kriya Yoga to many; this brought a scientific, physical and spiritual technique for becoming closer to God, acting in service to humanity and developing balance and harmony in life.

While in California, he became a close friend of Luther Burbank, who also walked in the light and whom Yogananda referred to as the "American

---

[5] Richard N. Sheldon, *Dag Hammarskjold* (New York: Chelsea House Publishers, 1987). pp. 14, 17.

Saint." Burbank recognized the light in plants and all of nature and was able to communicate with them, aiding them in their growth. Plants themselves are aware of and receptive to divine energy. An example was Burbank's talking to cactus plants, as he said, "I often talked with plants to create a vibration of love," and he would say to the cacti, "You have nothing to fear. You don't need your defensive thorns. I will protect you."[6] It is most interesting to note that these hardy desert plants gradually developed into thornless cacti. Burbank used his love and light energy also on other vegetables, fruits, and flowers.

While in the United States, Yogananda started a magazine in which he wrote interpretations of the New Testament. At one point, when he asked Christ for guidance in this, the light within became so strong that he was able to see a materialization of Jesus who shared the Holy Grail with him. Several years later Yogananda was guided to spend time in the Mojave Desert where he translated the Bhagavad Gita.

Although Yogananda's body died, it remained pure, with no sign of decay, for at least twenty days after his death. The light fully permeated the physical form.

The Peace Pilgrim is another light being. Is it not wonderful to see love truly expressed by one who is not only willing, but who desires to release all physical and material ties to be free to "walk the

---

[6] Paramahansa Yogananda, *The Autobiography of a Yogi* (Los Angeles: Self-Realization Fellowship, 1969), p. 361.

talk" for peace? It was so with the Peace Pilgrim, who was deeply aware of the lighted path that unequivocally directed her on her life's mission. At approximately age 50 in 1953, Peace began her cross country walking pilgrimage through the United States, eventually traveling to Mexico, Canada, Alaska, and Hawaii. Twenty-eight years later she completed her mission, for this lifetime, of 30,000 miles (25,000 on foot).

These illumined and special people bring great light and awareness into many hearts—and, as we, as individuals grow more and more into the light awareness, so will all the world. As the "Christophers" say, the light of one small candle can light the world.

The Peace Pilgrim had much to offer in truth and sincerity; light opened the door for her to see her path of service and love, as it can open doors for all humanity if we wish it and open the way to receive.

Light (truly) touched Peace to the depths of her being as her philosophy proves. She chose to overcome evil with good, to return love for any hurtful action that might be targeted toward her, to be killed rather than kill. One of her statements regarding forgiveness clearly demonstrates her expression of light/love, as, "I do not even need to forgive people, for I harbor no animosity. If they do evil things I feel compassion for them because I know they have hurt themselves. I hope they will be sorry because I want them to be healed."[7] We might say

---

[7] Peace Pilgrim, *Peace Pilgrim* (Santa Fe, NM: Ocean Tree Books, 1982), p. 143.

the basis of all the Pilgrim's philosophy and active
life is: "The way of peace is to overcome evil with
good, falsehood with truth, hatred with love."[8]

It is really amazing what one can accomplish
when filled with the understanding and awareness of
love and light. It can change our lives and the lives
of others, hence the entire world if we would continue to express this Divine Energy in spite of seeming
blocks that occur in our lives. We must remember
that such challenges are for growth so we can
strengthen our life/love actions and attitudes.

The average person may not elect to take a several thousand mile march, even if it's for peace.
However, each one of us has our own path to find
and to follow. The light will direct us in the right
direction.

Meditate in silence, open your "eyes" to that
beam of light that is for you; then follow it with no
fear, no stress, no pain. As Peace Pilgrim often said,
"Peace, be still—Peace, Peace."

Although it is most interesting and uplifting to
learn of our great well-known artists, spiritual masters, composers and the like, and to recognize their
radiance of light, we must not ignore the beauty,
joy, and light that radiates from the "every-day" person. A small child, for instance, may express unconditional love toward an animal, a flower, the stars,
while effusion of light flows out, in, and around the
child. Those who have "eyes to see" may recognize
this same Divine Light in a laborer who enjoys his
tasks and sets a goal for his creative workmanship.

[8] *Peace Pilgrim*, p. 97.

There is a story of two men who were working with cement blocks. A passer-by spoke to the first one and asked what he was doing. With a sigh and grunt, the workman replied, "I'm dragging these stones up a hill and piling one on top of the other." The passer-by walked on and came to the next laborer who was working with the same blocks. He, too, was asked about his work. As his face lit up with a smile, he replied, "Oh, I'm building a cathedral!" How different our perspective of life can be when we acknowledge the light in all we do, and let it shine.

Another interesting story reveals how the power of light can change our perception of a person when we allow ourselves to "see" with eyes of light. Dr. Gerald G. Jampolsky, a psychiatrist, writer, and lecturer, was preparing to give a lecture one night while in California. As he was about to leave for the lecture hall, there came a knock at the door of his hotel room. Upon opening the door, he met with a young, bedraggled and smelly teenager who said he had hitchhiked from Virginia to see Dr. Jampolsky, as he had seen him on TV and felt guided to make this contact. The young man stated that he did not know why he was led there except for the light he had seen in Dr. Jampolsky's eyes which drew him without any doubt, to his presence. Dr. Jampolsky explained he could not spend time with him until his lecture was over, and he seemed rather annoyed at this interruption. When they did get together, neither knew what to say; Dr. Jampolsky then suggested they meditate together. While doing so, he received an inner message pointing out to him the need this young man had to meet him, because of the great light and love he saw in his eyes. The message he received was, "Your gift to him is to demonstrate total acceptance to him, something he has never in his life experienced."[9] At that moment Dr. Jampolsky embraced the youth; a healing was received by both of them, and the smell and untidiness of the young man was no longer apparent to Dr. Jampolsky. Taking time to meditate allowed the power of the light to come forth and be expressed as love, which erased all negativity.

I could name thousands of illumined ones but it's also important to realize that there are many, many beings of light who work "behind the scenes," and many who appear to be just "average" human beings. Individuals with no apparent talents or gifts may pass you on the street and give a warm, happy smile. The light was there; the light shone forth. The light may appear to be hidden but could be doing the work in a quiet, unobtrusive way. We should greet everyone knowing that the light is there—the same light that is within you and me—whether it is being expressed or not. Perhaps it just needs a smile or touch from you to bring it forth.

Remember that the light shines forth on all levels. The only differences are expressed due to mankind's own choosing. "The genius does not differ from other persons in his access to light, only in his confident acceptance of its effusions."[10]

---

[9] Gerald G. Jampolsky, *Love is Letting Go for Fear* (Berkeley, CA: Celestial Arts, 1979), p. 101.
[10] Eric Butterworth, *In the Flow of Life* (Castro Valley, CA: Unity Press, 1982), p. 41.

CHAPTER 10

LIGHT—A DOORWAY TO THE PAST

We see and feel the light around us and within; we recognize its guidance leading us upward, and we acknowledge the illumination of the "tunnel" light which has shone so brightly for many who have had a near death ehtly for many who have had a near death experience (NDE). Have we, however, in deep meditation, ever asked the light to guide us to a past life which might throw light on a present problem? We learn to search ourselves honestly on *this* dimension; can we not be just as willing to explore past relationships and experiences which can bring light to today's challenges? So often we walk blindly on our present path, being limited in our understanding of "problems" and not being cognizant of the reason and purpose for the life we are now living.

So, after considering many phases, purposes and interpretations of the light, let it guide us into

previous lives so we can gain insight into current
problems and relationships that may be causing
disruptions in our lives. If you are going through an
extremely traumatic situation and cannot find a reason for it, or solution to it, then it might be to your
advantage to be courageous enough to delve
deeply into a previous lifetime—one whose karma
you are now experiencing. To see yourself "playing
another role" in the past can have a definite impact
on your present life. If we ask for the light to lead
us to truth, it will bring a greater understanding of
present situations. Once seen and felt, such things
can change and our acceptance turns the light on
karmic lessons that open our eyes to the purpose
for our place in the present.

Yes, it is true that we do need, at some point,
to release the past, but when we are faced with a
problem for which we see no cause, then this "tool"
can be a true help. If we ask in all sincerity, we will
arrive at that significant place which will have
meaning for us.

It is also worth mentioning at this point that
exploring past lives may not be a necessary step
for everyone. If we can truly release all negatives
of the past (including yourself and others), if we
can learn to forgive and accept forgiveness, if we
can send a blessing of light to all those present
conditions in our life, then we are free indeed to
step forward joyously with light and love in our
hearts. However, there has been much proof from
innumerable cases that by re-entering a past lifetime, we can resolve a negative situation, release
what had been a problem and thus make it possi-

ble to continue on our path with greater peace and understanding.

Total release of the past is important and would naturally be achieved when this "connecting" link has served its purpose; but perhaps we cannot do it until we have openly and honestly explored past events and actions on our part as well as of those around us, thus clearing the way for positive goals for our present and future. A good analogy is brushing dirt under the bed so it won't show. But it is there and must eventually be recognized and cleared out before our slate can be clean!

As we release the past into the light (see the "Seven Step Prayer" p. 23) it will either automatically free us of pain or it will show the meaning of the past, giving us a deeper awareness of the present, enabling us to conquer the present challenge.

Exploring past lives can often be exciting, informative, helpful, and many times, very beautiful. It may give us much spiritual insight. Follow the light. Now let us examine some ways we can use to explore our past.

First you need to meditate, and surround yourself in a bubble of light. Ask that God's light of truth and protection guide you into a time and space that can be meaningful for you. Release all fears and worries, and feel yourself engulfed in light. Feel yourself being lifted in and out of the present, and suddenly you will be there!

The first thing to do is to look around, try to sense where you are, *who* your are, and what the environment is showing you. Are there other people around? Who are they, and what kind of life is there? What are they wearing? Where are you? All of these questions and more will aid you in becoming acquainted with this period. If anything seems to bother you, just detach yourself and know that you are an observer, that this exploration has a purpose. Remember that the light is protecting you and enlightening your concept of the drama before your eyes. When you have seen and experienced all that is necessary at the time, ask your Higher Self to direct you back to the present.

You can do this regression by yourself. Oftentimes it is very helpful to have someone else guide you. The following is another and more detailed way to explore your past lives. Start with the same initial steps mentioned; put yourself into a relaxed and meditative state, just "let go," surround yourself in light and follow these steps. Picture yourself stepping into an elevator and pushing the "UP" button. As it reaches the top floor, open the door and see yourself stepping out on a beautiful, fleecy cloud. Lie on it and allow yourself to float calmly as you look all about you. You may at first look down at the earth and then gaze off into the distance as you let the cloud take you up higher and higher. Do this as long as it is comfortable. Then look down once more and you will faintly discern the planet earth. Now you are ready to make a descent. Ask that you be directed to the locale and time period that will give you the information for which you are searching. You will begin to descend gradually, as you see the globe rotating slowly. As you near the planet it will begin to slow down until you finally come too a time-space where you now put your feet on the ground. Then follow what was mentioned previously; look about, ask questions and see *yourself.* When it is time to return, again ask to be lifted back into the present.

This can be a tremendous experience. You might wish to do this for other people—not to direct them—but to look into their past. Do this *only with the other person's permission.* You may feel it necessary at some point to search into your own past with another individual. That could also be of help.

This regression can be used for eradicating negatives as well as to see your own progress. You have a chance to see previous talents and abilities which may still lie dormant within you. Each person has memories buried deep within, and a memory, at onne moment, may present you with a picture of a prior self and a life you've led. This present memory may often be confirmed in your regression experience. Thus by learning more of yourselves, your abilities, goals, and the like, it will help encourage your continuing progress on life's current path.

Many wonderful experiences can be received from this delving into the past, more than you realize. It does not imply a need to hold on to the past, but gives you a chance to review what has been, as a booster for the next step. Once you see it, and you receive helpful awareness from it, then it's time to release and move on.

Why do we sometimes feel strongly drawn to a particular country in a certain era? Do we not, at some point in life, feel a definite pull toward another person or have a strong negative reaction to someone we have just met? Such reactions and feelings can point to a past occurrence with associations and perhaps places; and "going back" can (while letting the light lead you) aid in understanding, forgiving, and bringing more balance into the "now."

Many have been helped by such regressions, giving more light on the subject of our lives, pointing out the connection of lifetimes, and showing the continuity of our paths of growth. It is a release when we choose to travel back in time. We gain more understanding of a particular relationship, the stress of a special problem, and we gain more knowledge of who we are now, why we are here, and where we are presently on our path. Remember, though, we may alo see and re-live beautiful and heart-warming times and contacts.

Our life now is part of a continuous chain of events, for we remain the same soul entity, but "play" different roles as necessary for our growth. Life becomes exciting and meaningful as we delve more and more deeply into it, developing ever greater insights as we allow that inner spark to guide us to truth.

• • •

Although emphasis in this book has been on the light energy we use in this present lifetime, I should also acknowledge the greatness of this same light that can lead us to the future or "life after death" planes. Many have been led by the light into Near Death Experiences, where they go through a tunnel of light and enter the heavenly worlds. There they receive the great gift of contacts with beautiful beings, masters, angels, and often, the Christ; they are also exposed to beautiful beams of color, far beyond our vision on earthly planes.

Feeling the reality of such wonderful joy and heavenly peace makes it difficult for those from earth to return here. They are told by guides, however, that they have not yet completed their purpose in this life and therefore must return to finish their mission. When these individuals return to this life, they are completely transformed; their understanding and acceptance of life has made a definite change toward a spiritual direction and unquestionable faith.

When death gives up the body completely, the spirit-self moves on to other planes—such as the astral, mental, and even to higher planes. Where we go depends on the individual soul's level of consciousness; always, however, being guided by the Light. According to the soul's growth, the light may be recognized and accepted, or rejected if the soul is unwilling to "see." Many souls remain earthbound for quite some time after death, but there are others who willingly release themselves from this plane, and allow the light to guide them to higher planes of consciousness and experiences. The light may assist them in reincarnating on this earth level if such an experience is necessary. There are also many highly evolved entities who could continue moving forward to ever greater spiritual planes, but choose to accept the light's direction to return to Earth in order to serve and teach.

Whatever our path is—here or in the "Beyond"—we are presented the Divine Light of guidance which will be with us forever. There is no limit to what this great light, which began with the creation of life, can do for us!

CHAPTER 11

DEEPER AWARENESS

Awareness is knowing that you know. This awareness grows when we allow our own spark of light to lead the way. Awareness is a sensitivity—knowing that within you is the answer to every question. Within *you* is the potential for un you is the potential for ultimate growth. Human beings came into this world knowing everything. The knowledge is in your cells, but you may not know that you know. Plato said that human beings know everything, and that studying is really only remembering.

Awareness is seeing, hearing, touching, not only on a physical level, but also and more importantly, on the spiritual level. How truly aware are we of the significance and *intelligence* of every cell in our bodies? Each cell is a living entity—a complete trinity of body, mind and spirit. The All-Knowing Father resides in us—in every cell and atom. As we develop further awareness of this truth, we begin to feel more and more of Divine Spirit pulsating through us, and we see this Oneness of all life within the trees, flowers, animals, and each and every human being. Do we ever look deep into the center of a beautiful blossom (as we would look into our own eyes) to understand what truly created this bit of nature, to see what gave it color and life?

There are many blind people who do very ell without the help of a seeing eye dog, as they are sensitive to light vibrations. They have developed their other senses to the point where they are aware of approaching a certain object, or a walled area as opposed to an open field. They have developed sensory skills because of a need. The potential for greater sensitivity is always there, but it lies dormant until a great need calls it forth.

Awareness is "feeling" a person when someone approaches. Oftentimes we have an immediate aversion to someone, or we have a very positive reaction to them. It is as if we put forth invisible antennas which touch and record vibrations of people and objects. Often when we enter a house or particular room, we immediately sense "something" about it. We react. That is awareness. By realizing that we react, and watching our reactions, awareness increases.

When we develop "extended" vision, we will see or be conscious of many sights and impressions, many of which may be unpleasant. That is when we must learn to surround ourselves in a bubble of light that will protect us from negative emanations. It is for us to choose the many vibrational energies in the ethers around us. We may remain vulnerable to negativity, or we may decide to act on faith and apply the energies of light that will shield and protect us.

We must learn to discriminate between those things which need our attention and to which we may give service, and other situations which tend to control us. Once we are *in the light,* we know that we need not allow the negative thought forms and vibrations to influence us.

There are many ways to develop deeper awareness, to gain "inner" sight, to open the Third Eye. It is the *desire* for this growth that starts us on the path. Then we consider the motive, the reason that we wish to expand our centers of awareness. There are numerous ways to begin. For example, we can pick up our mail one day, without looking at the return address. We can hold it in our hands and try to get the "feel" of the vibrations. We all "receive" differently. Some may "see" inside the letter or see the name; others may have a sudden picture come to mind, or we just have a thought of the one who wrote the letter. When the telephone rings, try to sense who it is, not by guessing, but by being aware of that first subtle flash of thought, recognizing that intuitive impression for what it is. By not forcing, but merely "letting go," we can more readily know what we already know.

Many such exercises can lead to a greater awareness if they are done with a sincere motive and a desire for good to come forth. The opening of our centers can be a dangerous thing if used improperly. However, if we work to "open up" our spiritual consciousness for a truly pure purpose, then we will be in the Light, where there is no fear, no hesitation, only a strong impulse to continue climbing onward and upward. As long as we surround ourselves with the light and maintain this consciousness, we will be protected and strengthened. Whenever we sense anyone or anything trying to invade our thoughts and actions, we need to envelop them also in this Divine Light for their awakening as well. We must also remember that negativities can influence us only to the degree that we allow them.

There are many methods for developing this greater awareness. Some schools advocate sitting in front of a candle-lighted mirror, as this may aid us in seeing within. Others spend hours meditating and concentrating the light on the chakras to release the energies. Others find it most helpful just to sit in the Silence, asking for divine guidance. All ways are helpful. We each must find our own appropriate way. Visualization is very important in awareness growth. For example, we can "see" ourselves stepping out of the physical self and as we do this, a part of us actually extends itself outward. As this develops more and more, it becomes astral travel, and our astral body travels wherever we send it in our imagination. Remember, imagination is creative. In attempting any of these methods, we always place ourselves in the protective and uplifting light as that will guide us properly on our quest.

It is true that we study and learn a great deal during sleep, according to our level of growth. We can, if we wish (and it is always our choice), send forth the desire to develop greater awareness of these "during sleep" experiences that we may bring them back into conscious knowing.

Awareness of angels and/or other spiritual entities is possible as our inner seeing grows. Clairvoyants will "see"; others will merely "feel" presences. These abilities can be developed, not by force, but by keeping the sensory centers open for "awareness signs," by accepting and using whatever comes to us and, most of all, by sincerely desiring this growth and expansion of spirit.

Think, smell, taste and "see" other places and events. For instance, think of the ocean surf, then hear it; smell the salt water; see the courtyard of early Egypt, or something similar that may come to our memories. Let the light lead us on this chain reaction of memories. We can *believe* what we receive.

To become truly aware is to become truly spiritual. The intent must be to become aware of our Oneness with the Creator. If we really wish to start on this quest for awareness, it can be an exciting adventure. There is nothing dull about spirituality.

The choice is yours. Do you want to live more deeply, more fully? Then turn on the spark within and start your climb up the mountain of LIGHT!

CHAPTER 12

UNDERSTANDING
CREATION

Sound came first. "And God said, 'Let there be Light, and there was Light" (Genesis 1:3). The Creator spoke and filled the Universe with Light; then Light brought forth diverse forms of life, all of which are continuously evolving. Creation was, and is, both physical and spiritual, and both are moving forward in growth and light awareness. As with everything, there are always different theories. However, the general consensus of opinion from archaeologists, other scientists, and historians is that the beginning of this planet was somewhere in Central Asia and is several billion years old. It is difficult to imagine the beginning when Earth was without form or substance. A picture presents itself of Pure Spirit, filling and being the omniverse. Spirit-God then moved, stirred, and activated the ethers, dispersing the atoms of the universe which then formed the waters and the form of the Earth. Once again, we see that everything is a part of the whole, as the atoms that make up Earth and human beings are the same as those that are in the furthest reaches of the universe; as above, so below.

God, being Light, then projected forth a part of Himself when He proclaimed that there would be Light and so it was. This light, then, is a part of Earth and all life forms thereon. The Creator Himself manifested forth as Pure Light and knew it to be good and perfect. This outpouring (a breathing out of the Holy Breath) undoubtedly took many eons and each was called a "day." As the Holy Breath withdrew, there was darkness and this was called night, or the period of rest (the "seventh day") after the creating or manifesting forth.

As Earth was first formed, it was not the solid mass as we know it to be today, but it was more luminous and misty. According to many teachings, the first life developed about forty million years ago—those forms also being light and transparent. It has been said that although Earth was created several billion years ago, the light of the original so-called fireball, which created the big bang theory, can still be detected. The light is still there.

The "lights in the firmament" as mentioned in the creation story give us the signs and seasons of the year. The Wise Men of ages past followed the light of the stars and this liight has given indications of spiritual occurrences. It has also stimulated our curiosity into the mysteries of the heavens. Not only did the light create as God spoke the word, but it filled all heavenly and earthly bodies with this same light. This light is still with us and is continually creating. It has filled human beings with light and it is now our prerogative to "see" this luminous energy and to apply it to all paths of life.

There is so much symbology to understand regarding the beginning of time and our beginnings. For example, what is the symbolism of the Garden of Eden? The Hebrew word for the Garden is "Ganheden." "Gan" means an organized sphere of activity, a world. The word "Heden" indicates a time, an age or an eternity. So, although there ay have been a literal, physical Garden of Eden in Asia, this can also refer to a spiritual state of consciousness in a certain time-space.

As we allow Light to show us the way to interpret these many symbolic descriptions, let us think of the meaning of good and evil. Spiritual "man" was created in the image of God, but the physical human being individualized in material form and started to evolve through the material world, thus becoming aware of the *less than good*. Once we began to eat (take into our consciousness) from the tree of the knowledge of good and evil, this "evil" was then reinforced by our very thought. The question often arises as to how we first began to think of the meaning of evil. Perhaps as the Divine Spark (mankind) descended more and more into the gross elements of life, the original awareness of our divine self left us and we became enmeshed in matter, accepting it as evil rather than seeing it as good. We failed to see and feel the beauty and love of Spirit, and were no longer in the "Garden Consciousness." We had removed ourselves from that state of love, serenity, and light.

So it is with the story of the "fall." Many cultures and religions tell stories of human beings falling out of light into darkness. Milton, in "Paradise Lost," used this as his theme; in Greek mythology, the Titans exercised too much individual power and so were cast out, or "fell"; and in Persia and ancient India there are also stories of misusing power and thereby "falling." The "fall" is really nothing but entering the pathway of evolutionary progress, the beginning of self-directed paths. The phrase "cast out" or "fell" merely signifies our following our own will power, our own choice of direction, "falling" away from the light from which we emanated forth.

The "as above, so below" principle is evident here, as we can parallel the evolving of our planet Earth to that of the human species, sometimes stepping away from the awareness of God, perceiving the so-called evil to the extent that it keeps us out of the "Garden of Eden." And are we not constantly creating, from our own light, the things of the world?

There are many interpretations of truth, but we must always keep in mind that we should search for the story behind the story in all myths, legends, and parables that come down to us through the ages. In all myths and imaginings of mankind, there has to be some element of truth in the ethereal substance out of which the images come forth. Our thoughts are creative, and it is *light that gives them substance.* Watch for that which we create; watch for the symbology in our lives, and allow the Light of Truth to interpret the inner meanings to aid us in our growth.

CHAPTER 13

SEEING THROUGH THE WINDOWS OF THE SOUL

Since we are "children of the light," then we will truly see with the eyes of the Master. Undoubtedly a change is necessary from our accustomed way of seeing things to a new perception. We must not merely sg things to a new perception. We must not merely see with the physical eye but must behold the light with our inner vision.

Let's think about eyes. It is said that the eyes are the windows of the soul; that they are a link between our outer world and our Higher Self. Even animals can see with this inner light; they can see forms of life beyond the material level. If we accept this ability to see on a higher plane, then we must allow this inner light to shine through to increase our recognition of Truth in people and situations. This is as a Master sees.

The physical eyes are representative of the way we feel within, and the way we view the outer world. It has been said that those who are far-sighted feel troubled or dissatisfied with the NOW. They do not perceive things nearby, i.e., the present, but the wish to project into the future. As for those who are near-sighted, they are unable to see distances— the future; perhaps they are fearful of it. They are more realistic, wanting to see what is near, but not daring to look into the beyond. Those with astigmatism put up barriers, not being satisfied with either the now or the future. Physical problems are always, to some degree, a reflection of something within that is out of balance. The outer always mirrors the inner. Therefore, eye problems are almost forcing us to take an in-depth screening of ourselves to determine how we are mentally viewing our world.

There is a simple light exercise that may help to clear up eye problems. Visualize the light from your own light center going up to and filling your eyes. Do this for five minutes, three times a day. This awareness of working with the light should help to raise your consciousness, which is important when doing physical healing.

There are various levels of seeing, if we would but "open our eyes." If we allow the light of truth to enter our field of awareness, we would find there is much, much more to learn, not only on higher dimensions, but on this physical plane also. When the third eye opens, angels, devic beings, and much in the ethereal world becomes visible to us. We can help develop this by again "sending" our inner light to the third eye area. Light clears the way of any obstruction; it opens the path.

"The light of the body is the eye: if therefore thine eye be single, thy whole body shall be full of light" (Matthew 6:22). If we see with the "single eye," we are seeing One, not many. The Masters see the Oneness of all creation, at the same time recognizing the many individual sparks that we are—sparks of the One Divine Light. We must learn to grow beyond this one level so that the Master Self within can grow to ever higher dimensions and then see with ever greater brightness and luminosity. There is no finality in this growing process. The light that leads us onward is ever glowing and moving ahead. It the light that will never dim or fade out.

We must remember that we have a Super Being within us, and we must open the door, we must open our eyes and let this Higher Self express outwardly. We must be the light for the world. As mentioned in the introduction, the planet Earth is our present home and we have a responsibility to try to bring to it harmony, peace, and love. Although this is our home, we must not restrict our use of and receptivity to light to this plane only. This great light enables to see into other worlds, to recognize angel beings and others of the spiritual realms. The light reaching us from other worlds is the same as the light we send to far off galaxies and beings. The more we send and receive, the greater our soul's vision becomes.

The things that we perceive in this world are facts, and seem to be reality to us of limited vision.

However, when we truly see, we will know the divine purpose underlying all, and will recognize this world as an illusion and not the Truth of our life.

Who is a Master? Anyone and everyone who knows and accepts the divinity within. When this is truly known, you will not see separation; you will see the spiritual self of all beings, the spiritual self of the planet, and the Oneness. Let the Master in you shine through your eyes—the windows of the soul. Walk as a child of the light.

Conclusion

It is not only interesting, but uplifting, to understand the true meaning of light and what it can do for us. It adds to our realization of Oneness when we learn to appreciate the philosophies of other cultures and faiths.

Light can do wonders for us, as Light is, itself, a wonder. It is a small word, but it is unlimited in its essence. It has so much to tell us and has great significance throughout the omniverse; it is the basis of all life, yet it has many interpretations.

It is helpful for us to understand the reality of light in all dimensions of living, in all forms and in our own growth process. Learning about the various aspects of light, the scientific as well as the spiritual, aids us to better comprehend our being and to truly see the radiance within. It is hoped that the more we learn about this great reality, the more we will follow its path, and the greater will be our recognition of and thankfulness for it.

As we grow in deeper awareness of this most important part of our life, we will find our opportunity to serve by assisting others toward their spiritual advancement. To see the workings of the light energy in all people helps us to be less judgmental, to be more open and compassionate.

Many of our teachings, philosophies and evolutionary trends point the way to a wonderful new beginning for our planet and all of humanity. A tremendous change is said to be scheduled to take place by the year 2000, or before. When this happening occurs, we will receive greater awareness of this tremendous gift of light that we, and the entire planet, have been given. It will shine forth and we will be receptive to it!

I end this book with a blessing to all who read, absorb, and share this great gift that is here for all life—forevermore.

Bibliography

Academic American Encyclopedia. Danbury, CT: Grolier Electronic Publications, 1995.

Aivanhov, Omraam Mikhael. Light is a Living Spirit. Los Angeles: Prosveta, 1987.

Babbitt, Edwin S. The Principles of Light and Color. New York: Carol/Citadel, 1980.

Baha'u'llah. The Book of Certitude. Wilmette, IL: Baha'i Publishing Trust, 1931.

———. Gleanings from the Writings of Baha'u'llah. Wilmette, IL: Baha'i Publishing Trust, 1952.

———. Kitab-I-Iquan: Agda's: The Most Holy Book. Wilmette, IL: Baha'i Publishing Trust, 1993.

Bodhananda, Swami. Lectures on Vedanta Philosophy. New Rochelle, NY: Knickerbocker Press, 1928.

Bucke, Richard Maurice. Cosmic Consciousness. New York: E. P. Dutton, 1969.

Butterworth, Eric. In the Flow of Life. Castro Valley, CA: Unity Press, 1982.

The Dhammapada. Trans. U. Dhammajoti. Benares, India: The Maha-Bodhi Society, 1943.

Eadie, Betty J. And Curtis Taylor. Embraced by the Light. Placerville, CA: Gold Leaf Press, 1992.

Foundation for Inner Peace. A Course in Miracles. New York: Foundation for Inner Peace, 1975.

Fundison, Barbara. Course in Miracles Concordance. Farmingdale, NY: Coleman Graphics, 1983.

Gawain, Shakti. Living in the Light. New York: Bantam, 1993.

Gottlieb, Simcha. Let There be Light. New York: Merkos Linyonei Chinuch, 1987.

Hall, Manly Palmer. The Blessed Angels. Los Angeles: Philosophical Research Press, 1980.

Hammarskjold, Dag. Hammarskjold. New York: Chelsea House, 1987.

Hauck, Louise P. Beyond Boundaries. Nevada City, CA: Blue Dolphin, 1993.

Hodson, Geoffrey. The Brotherhoood of Angels & of Men. Wheaton, IL: Theosophical Publishing House, 1982.

————. Fairies at Work and at Play. London: Theosophical Publishing House, 1925.

Holy Bible: King James Version. Oxford and New York: Oxford University Press. n.d.

Humann, Harvey. The Many Faces of Angels. Marina del Rey, CA: DeVorss, 1987.

Jampolsky, Gerald G. Love is Letting Go of Fear. New York: Bantam, 1984.

Kitagawa, Joseph M. "The Eightfold Path," in Great Religions of the World. Ed. Gilbert M. Grosvenor. Washington, DC: National Geographic Society, 1971.

Lee, Kremis More. Poughkeepsie Journal. December 1994. Published by Poughkeepsie Division of Gannet Satellite Information Network, Inc., 85 Civic Center Plaza, P.O. Box 1231, Poughkeepsie, NY 12602.

Levi. The Aquarian Gospel of Jesus the Christ. Marina del Rey, CA: DeVorss, 1972.

Liberman, Jacob. Light: Medicine of the Future. Santa Fe: Bear & Co., 1991.

Medicine Eagle, Brooke. Buffalo Woman Comes Singing. New York: Ballantine, 1991.

Morris, Richard. Light:From Genesis to Modern Physics. New York: Macmillan, 1979.

Newhouse, Flower A. The Kingdom of the Shining Ones. Escondido, CA: The Christward Ministry, 1955.

Peace Pilgrim. Peace Pilgrim. Santa Fe: Ocean Tree Books, 1982.

Peck, M. Scott In Search of Stones. New York: Hyperion, 1995.

Ramacharaka, Yogi. Bhagavad Gita. Chicago: Yogi Publishing Society, 1935.

Regush, Nicholas. The Human Aura. New York: Berkeley, 1974.

Schweitzer, Albert. J. S. Bach. New York: Dover, n.d.

———. The Quest of the Historical Jesus. New York: Macmillan, 1968.

Sheldon, Richard. Dag Hammarskjold. New York: Chelsea House Publishing, 1987.

Spaulding, Baird. Life and Teachings of the Masters of the Far East. 4 vols. Marina del Rey, CA: DeVorss, 1924.

Tanner, Florice. Mystery Teachings of World Religions. Wheaton, IL: Theosophical Publishing House, 1973.

Yogananda, Paramahansa. Autobiography of a Yogi. Los Angeles: Self-Realization Fellowship, 1969.

Zajonc, Arthur. Catching the Light. New York: Bantam, 1993.

INDEX

ABOUT THE AUTHOR

Mary Bassano has a background in music and social work, and has published a book titled "Healing with Music and Color." She is deeply involved with metaphysical and esoteric studies, and is a member of the International Church of Ageless Wisdom, where she earned her D.D. For many years she has given workshops in music and color, has taught metaphysical classes, and given lectures.